SOUTH ATLANTIC OCEAN

Cape Dolphin

Foul Bay

Middle Bay

MT ROSALIE

PORT SAN CARLOS

SAN CARLOS

SOUND

Grantham Sound

DOUGLAS

SALVADOR

RINCON GRANDE

PORT LOUIS

JOHNSON'S HARBOUR

GREEN PATCH

Berkeley Sound

TEAL INLET

BIG MT.

MT SIMON

NO·MANS LAND

MT USBORNE

MT WICKHAM

SMOKO MT.

MT KENT

MT CHALLENGER

BLUFF COVE

STANLEY

FITZROY

DARWIN

GOOSE GREEN

LAFONIA

WALKER CREEK

Choiseul Sound

EAST FALKLAND

LIVELY I.

Lively Is

Adventure Sound

Low Bay

Lively Sound

NORTH ARM

Bay of Harbours

BLEAKER

Bleaker I.

Sea Lion Is.

● SETTLEMENTS
— ROADS
- - - TRACKS

0   5   10   15   20   25miles

The Bird Man

ABOUT THE BOOK

For nearly 20 years, Ian Strange has devoted himself to the preservation of wildlife in an area where many species are in danger. He has won the rare victory of creating island paradises for birds on the Falkland Islands in the South Atlantic.

A brilliant painter and photographer, and a keen observer of wildlife, Ian Strange endorses positive conservation to improve and develop man's environment. He has organised a series of tours of the Islands which have proven that wildlife preservation can be as profitable as the industries which threaten wildlife.

The story of his personal discovery and explorations of the Falklands and its wildlife inhabitants, his success in winning the attention of bureaucracy and commercial interests, is an unusually encouraging one in the field of conservation.

ABOUT THE AUTHOR

Ian Strange is universally known in Britain and America as the Bird Man. His own articles in the *New York Times* and other American newspapers and articles and television programmes about his work have made him a household name.

He was born in England and spent part of his childhood in the house which Sir Peter Scott eventually made the headquarters of the Wildfowl Trust. He was trained as an artist and is now one of the finest living painters of birds. He first settled in the Falkland Islands in 1959 and has dedicated himself to studying and protecting their wildlife ever since.

GOOD READ

The Bird Man

An Autobiography

IAN STRANGE

GORDON & CREMONESI

Designed by Heather Gordon

Set in 12 on 13 pt 'Monotype' Garamond
and printed in Great Britain
by W & J Mackay Limited, Chatham

ISBN 0–86033–015–X

Gordon Cremonesi Ltd
New River House
34 Seymour Road
London N8 0BE

Contents

List of Illustrations

Colour Plates

Black and White Plates
(between pages 44 and 45)

During gales on Beauchêne Island.

The main colony of King penguins at Volunteer Point nesting with a group of Gentoo penguins.

A Johnny Rook, an endangered species. The Falklands may be one of their last breeding grounds.

(between pages 140 and 141)

A King cormorant in full breeding plumage.

An adult pair of Rockhopper penguins with their chick.

A Gentoo penguin feeding its chick.

Black-browed albatross coming in to feed their young on Bird Island.

A Brown Hooded or Pink Breasted gull (*Larus maculipennis*).

The endangered Johnny Rooks on Beauchêne Island.

The author looking out over the huge colony of albatross and penguin on Jason Island.

A Black-browed albatross on its nest with a penguin nearby.

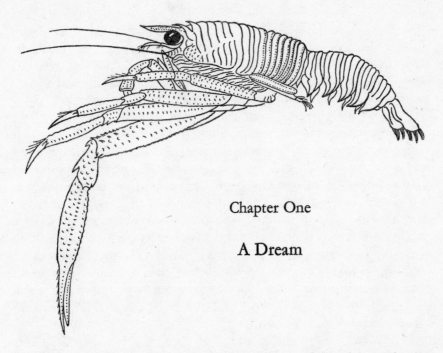

Chapter One

A Dream

As we approached the shoreline, a light breeze from the north-west was coming off the island, carrying with it the unmistakable stench of guano from a penguin rookery. Fortunately the swell had subsided during the night and there was now every chance that I should be able to get ashore without difficulty. I was tense with excitement at the prospect of landing on the island at last. We were heading for a point on the coast at which the sheer rockface rose only some fifteen feet from the sea; this seemed the only place on that side of the island that offered us any hope of landing. However, as we rounded a bluff that had hidden the proposed landing site from view, my hopes suddenly dropped, for the swell, though gentle, was moving several feet up and down the cliff face. Still, as we had been lowered in the whaler over the side of the naval patrol vessel that had brought me to the island, I had been told that we had the ship's best coxswain on board; a few minutes later I was to see proof of this.

As the swell reached its highest point, the coxswain manoeuvred the whaler close to the rockface, and then the rest was up to me. After jumping I clung to the narrow ledge, hoping that gravity would not get the better of me; but the knowledge that I was at last on the island overcame my fears, and in a few minutes I had made the climb to the top.

I had come to the island specially to look for fur seal, since it was reputed that here was the largest colony of them in the Falklands. Some distance from where I had landed I stood looking over the stained and polished rock. It was December, when the seal should have been at the height of their pupping, but there were no seal. I was utterly disappointed, but my disappointment was soon to be overcome by the discovery of something else.

The smell of penguins was even stronger now, and from where I was standing I could clearly pick out the calls of these birds and what sounded like the soft murmur of surf on the opposite coast. Walking over the rise I found the penguins, rockhoppers, nesting together with black-browed albatross. Among the mass of rock slabs that covered this part of the island were many thousands of both species, but it was what I could see in the distance, about half a mile off, that took my breath away. Stretching along the opposite coast and disappearing out of sight to the northern end of the island was a vast rookery of albatross and penguins, larger than any other I had seen in the archipelago.

The sound that I had thought was surf came in fact from this rookery. So tightly packed were the nesting birds that it would have been impossible to have walked through them without treading on nests, eggs or the birds themselves. How many birds were there, I wondered—one million, two million, perhaps even more? The seal had gone, but this vast rookery of birds was quite sufficient to warrant the island's being given reserve status. I decided that one of my main jobs on the island must be to establish just how large the rookery was, making this a feature of my report.

Before the evening light started to fail I established camp close to an area of tussac grass that covered a large portion of the island. As darkness came the murmur of sound from the rookery of birds increased dramatically, until it resembled the sound of some great waterfall. Then, quite suddenly, above this background sound I heard other calls, and saw against the paler western sky dark shapes twisting and turning quickly as they flew above the tussac. It was then that I knew that the island was also used by large populations of petrels. By 2 a.m. most of them had descended to their nesting burrows and the ground issued forth the most weird assortment of calls. In another two hours dawn would begin to break over the island and these birds would again be leaving for the open sea.

Before crawling into my tent to get some much needed sleep I watched the lights of the naval patrol vessel as she steamed back and forth, charting by star set the exact position of the island. Then I slept and dreamed.

For more than four days now the trawler had been slowly moving from north to south and back again. On coming within a few miles of the islands she would turn and make her way back, then later return again. Day and night she worked, at night her position being marked by the floodlights fitted on the back of her slipway. That I had bothered to climb to the top of the high cliff late at night, just to see if she was still working, was rather ridiculous, for I knew that such vessels, costing many thousands of pounds a day to operate, had to work round the clock. What nationality she was I had no idea, but I knew she would be collecting food for some protein-hungry nation. They would be working under licence—what many called "controlled fishing"—but at whose expense? It was January, and we had been spending a lot of time on the rock-hopper penguin colony trying to establish why the birds were getting later in their breeding cycle. One thing we had established was that the adult birds were now spending much longer at sea before returning with feed for their young. Had some biological change taken place in the food chains? Twenty years ago we would have said "Yes, very probably". Now the cause was staring us in the face! Some years ago all seal colonies in the islands had been declared reserves of special value; gone at last were the dangers from sealing. But owing to economic pressures the authorities had then issued larger catch quotas to the fishing fleets, extending to include the forms of "krill" (phosphorescent shrimp-like organisms) in the range of marine life that could be taken. Within a short space of time the fur seal population had fallen, and now the same was happening to the bird colonies. I was not sure which was worse: this slow starvation or the disaster we had witnessed the previous year, when one of the mammoth "oil flubbers" used for storing oil from the offshore drilling bases had broken loose in a storm. There had been oil spills before, but this time several thousand tons of crude oil had been lost and tens of thousands of penguins, cormorants and albatross had perished.

I think it was the call of a caracara (a species of hawk) that actually woke me. Outside the tent the early morning air was warm and still and the clear green sea an oily calm; the familiar surf-like noise came from the rookery. I suddenly wondered about the dream: why the things it portrayed happened, and whether they would happen here. I had a feeling that they probably would, but when? In ten, fifteen or twenty years' time; who was to know?

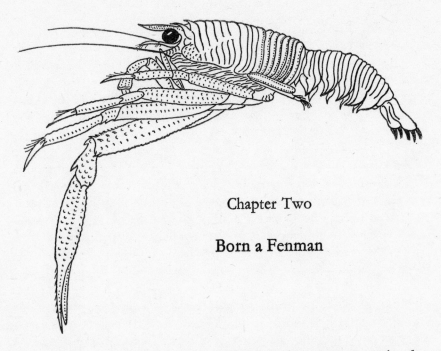

Chapter Two

Born a Fenman

It is said that some of the most vivid memories a person retains date from about the age of six. Certainly I can most clearly recall being taken for walks at this age, from Market Deeping in Lincolnshire (where I was born) to the home of my grandparents Strange, at Peakirk a few miles away. Although I believe we made these journeys in order to have Sunday lunch or tea at Peakirk, it is not the meals that I remember, but what I saw on the way to and from them. One such journey, made in spring, when flood waters lay over the fields, remains foremost on my memory. Standing on a small humpbacked bridge close to Peakirk, we had looked along the flooded dyke towards Crowland Bank and watched herons standing in the very still waters. The willow trees that dotted the landscape also left their impression, for in my mind's eye I can still see them marking the boundaries of flooded fields and ditches. Close to the house at Peakirk were osier beds from which basket makers obtained supplies of pliable willow stems, and among these beds were waterways inhabited by swans, coots and duck. The place fascinated me, and it was always a great treat to be allowed to stop and peer through a gap in the boundary hedge into this wild spot.

The house at Peakirk, The Goshams, once a hunting lodge owned by the Duke of Buccleuch also remains vividly in my memory. In particular, I remember its thick stone walls and reed-thatched roof; the smell of stored apples and homemade wine; and my grandfather's study with its mass of books and store cupboards, which I imagined held all manner of treasures. Oddly, I remember little of the house at Market Deeping or of my grandfather.

Both my mother's and my father's parents were keenly interested in wildlife, natural beauty and art. My mother's parents came from Keswick in Cumberland, which no doubt had some bearing on the love I developed of hills and mountains. However, while both sides of the family helped mould my interests, I believe it was my grandfather Strange whom I most took after in this respect. An amateur naturalist possessed of artistic talents, he maintained the grounds at Peakirk as a small bird reserve and for some years was part owner of the Monk's Wood Reserve at Abbots Ripton near Huntingdon.

Unfortunately, my father's work took us away from Market Deeping while I was still young. But at every opportunity I returned to Peakirk, spending most of my school holidays in that area and following my growing interest in wild life. Situated on Crowland Bank a short distance from Peakirk were two farms owned by second cousins: Sissons and the Borough Fen Decoy. I spent several summers at Sissons, helping out on the farm; but it was the Decoy farm that interested me most.

The Borough Fen Decoy, built about 1670, lies hidden in some twenty acres of woodland, a short distance from Crowland Bank. When I first visited it, it was still a place where duck were caught for the London markets. Everything about the Decoy fascinated me: its history, the 300 year-old workings, and the method of catching duck by enticing them from a central pond into covered waterways or "pipes". Using a specially trained dog, the decoyman, Billy Williams, whose ancestors had operated the Decoy since it was built, would exploit the curious behaviour of ducks towards predators. Overlapping screens along the side of the pipe allowed the dog suddenly to appear and then disappear before the ducks. Feeling secure on the water and curious of this apparent predator, they would follow the dog as it "retreated" along the banks of the covered ditches. At a certain point the decoyman would appear, seeming to block the ducks' escape route back to the pond. At this they flew on up the narrowing pipe until they were trapped in a special tubular net at the end.

In those days Peter Scott spent a lot of time at the Decoy, watching duck and painting; and I remember the great pleasure it gave me when I was shown round the house and saw some of Scott's pictures. Little did I then realise that in a few years the Decoy would be leased to the Severn Wildfowl Trust, for the study and ringing of duck, and that our Peakirk home also would become a wildfowl refuge owned by the Trust. For me it was a very sad time when the Peakirk house was given up, but I thought it fitting indeed that Peter Scott and the Severn Wildfowl Trust should have taken it over.

During my school days we lived just outside Wolverhampton in Staffordshire, and, though we were close to the Shropshire border and had a distant view of the Welsh hills, the area in which we lived was suburban and I was never to become deeply attached to it. Besides, I had a lot of trouble from illness and twice had to spend long periods convalescing after bouts of rheumatic fever. At school, my best subjects were art, natural science and geography, and I was keen to make my career in the biological sciences. However, it was recommended that I make my way in art; and, since my advisers thought that it was only by a career as commercial artist that one could wield a brush and pencil and still make a living, I spent a year training at the Wolverhampton College of Art. This convinced me that commercial art was far from my vocation, besides which the prospect of having to work within four walls horrified me. Botanical illustration, which I did enjoy, gave me a glimmer of hope for combining art with the outdoor life, and this eventually took me to the Birmingham Botanical Gardens as a student during the day, and to Birmingham University and Technical College as an extra-mural student in the evenings.

In my spare time I took part in a number of outdoor activities in which, owing to the long periods of illness I had suffered while at school, I had previously had no real opportunity to participate. These activities—cycling, climbing and hiking—also offered travel, and before I was eighteen they had taken me over much of England and Wales and through a number of countries on the continent. This whetted my appetite to see and do more.

One way of doing this was to join the Forces, and, since I had grown up with the idea that I would spend some time in the Army, the time seemed right to join. My decision was influenced too by the fact that conscription was then still in operation. As I wanted to do something active and interesting, and not just serve time in a unit that was of no interest to me, I went to an Army recruiting centre and put my name down for service in the Independent Parachute Brigade. It is a move that I have never regretted. I became attached to a small unit involved in search and rescue, and as a result visited some interesting and remote areas of the Middle East.

After coming out of the Army, I spent a year at the Essex College of Agriculture, so as to obtain further qualifications fitting me for an occupation in which my love of outdoor life and the countryside would be able to play a part. Farming and horticulture were a natural interest, but even though I was now heading towards these professions I was still uncertain of what I wanted to do. While in Essex I worked on four farms, all of which happened to be situated close to the coastal marshes. Like the Fens, these regions fascinated me, and my early interest in this type of countryside and its bird life was reborn.

Like many who have developed a deep interest in bird life and its preservation, I went through a phase of being interested in wild-fowling and game shooting, and even trained two red setters for the purpose. Looking back, I am sure that this interest in wildfowling was stimulated mainly by a deeper interest in walking lonely marshes watching duck, geese and waders and listening to the dawn calls of these birds. At first it seemed rather ridiculous to do this for its own sake, so I went in the company of dog and gun. The few birds that I did shoot certainly were never valued for their meat; rather for the opportunity to view them at close quarters. This is borne out by the fact that, whenever I discovered that some other wildfowler had bagged an uncommon type of duck, I invariably asked to see the bird and to have its head, wings and feet!

One area of Essex that I came to know well was that around Kirby le Soken. There I became friendly with two brothers, John and David Digby. John was an expert on the birds found locally, was skilled at taxidermy, and owned an interesting collection of waterfowl. He and I went into partnership, farming a small acreage on his father's farm; but, although we worked hard for long hours, we were never very successful. Both of us were more interested in wildlife than in farming, and often our thoughts turned to ways and means of combining the two pursuits. At one time an island in the marshes came up for sale, and our thoughts were stretched to the limit in working out schemes for buying the island, farming part of it, and maintaining the rest as a wildfowl refuge. Eventually, and reluctantly, we gave up the idea as a pipe-dream, but now I know that, had we had the courage of our convictions, we could have found the means to follow that idea through.

Also while at Kirby le Soken, I met a girl called Irene Hutley, whose father farmed at the nearby village of Great Holland. We were both interested in fur-bearing animals—otters, marten, mink and foxes—and realised that we could indulge our interest in a commercially viable way by starting a fur farm. This we did; our friendship inevitably became closer; and, by the time we had established our own stocks of mink, we had decided to marry.

For a time we lived at Great Holland, but as the mink farm grew we were forced to decide whether we would restrict our interest in these animals or would move our stocks elsewhere, so as to be able to expand the farm and devote ourselves to it full-time. We were both quite keen to move from England if necessary, and even considered setting up in Iceland. However, while we were pondering the question the whole matter was suddenly answered in a letter from the Hudson Bay Company in London.

This informed me that a company in the Falkland Islands was thinking of establishing an experimental fur farm in the islands and was looking for a suitable person to start this project. Would I be interested? That the letter should have arrived just then was an amazing coincidence, and I lost no time in finding out more. On 13 September 1959 I accepted the position offered and Irene and I prepared for a new life 8,000 miles away.

By December we were on our way, aboard a vessel that every three months made the journey from London to the Falklands carrying supplies for the islanders and then returned to London with the islands' wool clip. On this occasion the ship carried in a special housing on deck some fifty mink, which were to form the nucleus of the new farm.

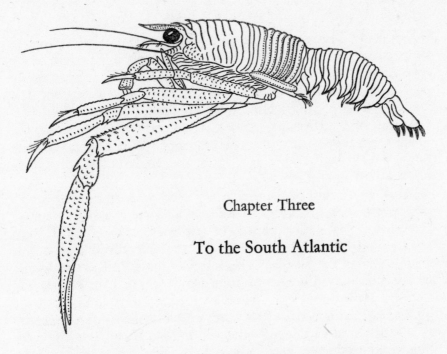

Chapter Three

To the South Atlantic

The journey from London to the Falklands took thirty days and passed uneventfully until we were just a day out of Port Stanley. Until then the sea had been a bright blue; but now it changed suddenly and dramatically to a deep greeny blue and teemed with life. There was a strong smell of seaweed and a sudden increase in the number of sea birds; all about us were species of petrel, gull and albatross.

Regrettably we made our approach to the islands at night: but on the day before Christmas Eve we stood on the deck of the charter vessel and took our first look at the Falkland landscape and the islands' small capital and only town, Port Stanley. The previous day I had had a strong feeling that I was going to like the islands; now, as I looked over this neatly laid-out town spread along the side of a hill and sloping down to the harbour front, I knew I did.

It was a beautiful day, and the red and green roofed buildings of the town added a splash of colour to the scene, setting off the rather sober greens, buffs and greys of the surrounding hills. Had we not known where we were, we might well have fancied that this remote British colony, lying just 400 miles north-east of Cape Horn in the South Atlantic's most turbulent seas, was part of the outer Hebrides. Indeed, though we knew the inhabitants were of British origin, we were amazed just how British they were. In addition, it was difficult to appreciate that these islands, which have a temperate climate and are classed as Sub-Antarctic, are only as far south of the equator as London is north. The prevailing winds are remarkably cool, and the smell they carry changes with their direction. The warmer summer winds blow from the land and carry the sweet fragrance of dwarf plants, grasses, sedge and fern; in contrast, the winds from the sea carry the rich aroma of seaweed from the huge offshore kelp beds. When it is calm, the predominant smell is of peat smoke from the houses.

Many who heard of the fur-farm project were puzzled about it: why establish a fur-farm on such an isolated group of islands? Except during the early periods of settlement, when the Falklands were ravaged by sealers and whalers, the only effective economic exploitation of the islands has been of their grasslands. First sighted by the Elizabethan navigator John Davis in 1592, the islands had not been settled until 1764, when the French under de Bougainville built a small settlement at Port Louis on East Falkland. De Bougainville introduced cattle, and until about 1860 these were the main livestock, producing beef, tallow and hides. By 1880, however, sheep farming, established soon after the islands were taken over by Britain in 1842, had become the Falklands' main industry. Today there are over half a million sheep there, and these are reared for their wool. The unsuitability of such sheep as meat producers has meant that the Falklands wool industry has always been left with a large surplus of old sheep, which when of no further use have been slaughtered and left to rot. Rather than waste this meat, it had been suggested, fur-bearing animals might be raised on it; and it was my job to investigate this possibility and establish an experimental farm to test its practicality.

The two main Falkland islands are East and West Falkland, and Stanley, which was our home for the next few years, is situated on East Falkland. The town has a population of about 1,000, and most of the islands' other inhabitants (also about 1,000) live in thirty or so sheep stations or settlements scattered about the group. Settlements on the two main islands are linked by tracks, over which horses or Land Rovers are used. Boats are sometimes used for linking Stanley with the outlying stations, but air travel is far more important. Using two Beaver float aeroplanes, the Falkland Islands Government operates an internal air service.

Shortly after my arrival in Stanley, I had the chance to go on one of the daily flights and get my first overall picture of the archipelago. Flying almost due west of Stanley, we crossed the centre of East Falkland, a rugged mass of small mountains the tops of which are broken by grey quartzite ridges. From these, long fingers of what from above look like scree point down into the shallow valleys, but flying low one sees that they are made up of huge angular blocks of stone. Known locally as "stone runs", they are a geological phenomenon peculiar to the Falklands. To the south of this mountain area and in sharp contrast to it is a vast plain of buff-coloured grass. The coastline of this plain is low and deeply indented, but the whole presented a rather sober and monotonous picture. Across the Falkland Sound, a strip of water dividing East from West Falkland, the land rises abruptly in small but impressive cliffs and the mountainous areas are more severely rugged than are the highlands of East Falkland.

The Falkland archipelago covers an area of about 4,620 square miles, and as we flew across the Sound at some 3,000 feet the sky was clear and we could see almost the whole group spread out below. The settlements, we saw, were placed close to harbours or creeks and varied in size from just two or three houses to twenty or more, the smallest settlements being those on the outlying islands. The whole scene was one of variety and interest, but what most fascinated me was the amazing number of islets and rocky stacks lying off the main coasts. These islands looked greener and more alive with wildlife than did the main islands, and at once I wanted to see them at much closer quarters and to discover more about them.

For the next two years the establishment and running of the fur farm took up almost all my time, and I had little opportunity for exploration. However, one of the islands that I had seen from the air lay only eight miles from Stanley, and just a few weeks after our arrival in the Falklands I made the first of many visits to Kidney, as it was called. The green cover of this and other small offshore islands I already knew to be tussac grass (*Poa flabellata*), but nobody seeing it from the air could possibly conceive how impressive it really is. Each plant forms a stool or fibrous base from which sprouts a mass of green leaf, often over four or five feet in height. Growing close together, the plants give dense cover and are difficult to move through, but form an important habitat for many birds and seal.

During my early days in the Falklands, I found that, although there was interest in, there was also considerable opposition towards, the fur-farm project. I took it that the opposition stemmed

from a concern for the islands' wildlife, but was puzzled when my
inquiries about bird life were treated in a rather negative manner;
also it seemed that little or nothing was known about it, except that
there were quite a number of penguins in the islands and large
quantities of wild geese, which farmers considered a pest. It was not
until I had been in the Falklands for quite some time that I discovered that worries about what would happen if any mink escaped
stemmed not from concern for the islands' bird life, but from fears
for the sheep. At one stage, I was even asked whether it would be
possible to farm the mink by letting them loose on one of the offshore islands, where they could live off penguins and other birds.
This horrified me, and showed me how casually the islanders viewed
their wildlife.

However, on a closer acquaintance with the islands' history, I
began to see why this was so. Until 1842, the islands had not been
permanently settled, and those who visited them came for sealskins,
whale, seal and penguin oil, or to replenish their vessels with wild-
bird eggs and game. The islands became a useful stopping-off place
for voyages farther south, and a place where pigs, goats and cattle
could be left to fatten on the rich vegetation, then later collected as
fresh meat. When people began to settle the Falklands, they did so to
exploit the islands' resources, and had little interest in anything that
was not of use to them. Further, their origins lay elsewhere and they
continued to maintain close relations with their mother country,
rather than develop a separate identity as Falklanders. I had the
feeling that few of the islanders saw the islands as a permanent
home, and that Argentina's continual claims to sovereignty over the
islands have contributed to this sense of impermanence. Thus it is
not surprising that when I arrived there were no wildlife reserves
and that little interest was shown in wildlife. What the islands had
in abundance was taken for granted, and few saw any need for
special protective measures.

Nonetheless, the islands did not go neglected by the outside
world, and before I had been in the islands for very long I had made
the acquaintance of a number of distinguished naturalists, including
Robin Leach, a young entomologist from British Columbia University; Dr Robert Cushman Murphy from the American Museum
of Natural History, an ornithologist of great distinction and
authority on birds of the South Atlantic; and Fergus O'Gorman, a
British Antarctic Survey seal biologist, who arrived in the islands
en route from fieldwork in Antarctica. Having spent some time

working on species of fur seal of the South American coasts, he was particularly anxious to discover more about the Falkland race and encouraged me to do some studies of these mammals, in which I had developed a special interest. One important aspect of this study was that of tag-marking seal for identification during future work; but, when I applied for permission to do this, I was refused, and politely told that I could not visit certain fur seal colonies. As a newcomer to the islands, I should have exercised greater diplomacy, for my request, innocent though it was, was open to misinterpretation. I realised that in future I should be more careful when proposing anything new or out of the ordinary. However, despite this setback and the fact that for over a year I was unable to take a full day off from the fur farm, by 1961 I had managed to carry out a number of surveys of fur seal and sealion.

On 1 January 1961, Irene and I had our first child, Shona, and just before the end of the year our second child, Sharron, was born. We were becoming increasingly fond of the islands and had begun to see our future as lying there. Thus, in the letter I sent home to England to announce Shona's birth, I wrote, "I honestly do not feel that I could return to England to live after being out in the Falklands, and if the mink farm fails I would almost certainly stay and live on one of the outer islands. Here are some wonderful experiences of living with wildlife, in places that are still practically untouched by man."

Certainly we had plenty to keep us occupied.

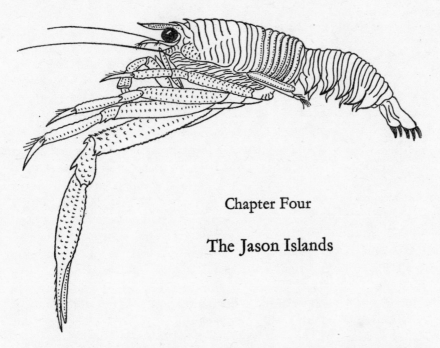

Chapter Four

The Jason Islands

Late in 1961 I began making arrangements to take leave from the farm, so that I could visit some of the more remote islands of the archipelago. In particular, I was attracted to the Jasons, which lie north-west of West Falkland and about which little was known. I discovered that, of the ten islands in this group, eight were owned by the Crown and had not been visited for many years, and two, Steeple Jason and Grand Jason, were privately owned and were stocked with sheep, though not settled. Once a year three or four men were taken out to these islands to shear, and it occurred to me that perhaps the boat that took them out could land me on one of the other islands, picking me up when the shearers returned. Everybody thought I was mad, saying that I would probably get stuck out there; and eventually it was arranged that I would go out to the sheep islands of Steeple and Grand Jason.

Some months before, I had met Roddy Napier and his wife Lilly. They lived and worked on West Point Island, which commands a view of the Jason group. Roddy was interested in birds and animals and, although a sheep farmer by profession, paid a lot of attention to the welfare of the birds on West Point. We were to become firm friends and he was later to be one of my main allies.

A bird in which I had become particularly interested was the striated caracara, locally known as "Johnny Rook", whose only

known breeding grounds are in the Falklands. Considered a pest by
many farmers, it appeared to be becoming rare; and there was thus
an urgent need to find out more about the bird and see what
measures might be necessary to ensure its survival. Roddy, who
considered the bird unfairly persecuted, told me that he thought the
largest populations of Johnny Rooks were to be found on the Jason
Islands, and this gave me added incentive to visit them.

Before I did so, I had a letter from the manager of Steeple and
Grand Jason islands asking me if I would check that his men were
not depleting to danger level the numbers of Johnny Rooks on
these islands. I was naturally very heartened by this attitude, which
suggested that the farmers were not as indifferent to wildlife as they
often appeared to be. Instead of flying out to meet the boat that was
to take me to the Jason Islands, I went aboard the Government
vessel *Philomel*, a small converted drifter of about 100 tons.
Obviously, this made for a more interesting journey; but I by no
means expected the voyage to do quite as much as it did to shape
my attitudes towards wildlife preservation.

The vessel was due to sail from Stanley at midnight on 23
February 1962—an unusual departure time for a ship with no radar
or aids for night navigation. At first I was puzzled by this, but it
turned out that it had been reported that a Russian whaling fleet was
working inside Salvador Waters in East Falkland, and that the
little *Philomel*, with a Government officer on board, was being sent
to intercept the fleet and deliver a note of protest. With weather and
sea conditions bad and deteriorating, our departure was delayed
until 6 a.m.; but, with tremendous seas running outside the harbour,
we made little headway even then and were forced to take shelter off
Kidney Island. While there, we received word that the Russian fleet
was moving out of Salvador Waters. Our voyage was now more
urgent, so we moved out, heading along the north coast.

At midday we sighted two whale catchers, one heading towards
the coast and another making her way out. Later a large factory ship
came into view, and an hour later we were closing in on this ship,
which, though still working, clearly was not going to move. There
had been speculation about why the ships were working so close to
shore; and, as the north coast of East Falkland was reputed to have
large sealion colonies, there were fears that seal were being taken.

As we approached the factory ship, which we estimated was a
vessel of 30,000 tons, I wondered how on earth our customs officer
was going to deliver the protest. With the swell still running, going

alongside would be a very dangerous business. Circling the huge ship, whose sides were higher than our mast, we found a tanker on her lee side, and, though this must have been about 10,000 tons, it was clearly safer to approach this smaller vessel. Work had ceased on board both ships and many faces were peering down at us, but, even though we made repeated indications that we wanted to come alongside to send someone aboard, no attempt was made to assist us. Twice we took *Philomel* in close to the tanker and threw our lines up, and twice they were deliberately let fall. The third time our lines were held, and, since it had been made clear that the customs officer wished to board, a rope ladder was lowered. I had been asked if I would take my camera and accompany the officer; but, the moment I made a move to follow him up the side, the ladder was whipped away, nearly causing me to fall between the two ships. Clearly the Russians were not going to have anyone aboard to record anything with a camera.

Shortly afterwards the customs officer was back, having delivered the Government's note of protest. Even this could not have been done if the Russians had not helped us, and I realised just how powerless we had been in our small boats and how vulnerable the Falklands were to such well-organised attacks on the whales and seals around the islands' coasts. How could such a small and isolated colony, 8,000 miles away from the "Motherland", operate any effective policing of her coastal waters?

Later we saw a whale surface, blow and dive. I wondered how long it would be before it was being hauled up the slipway of that factory ship. With the helicopters and sophisticated gear these ships use to find such mammals, what chance do these creatures have?

The following day the sea was calm and it was possible to follow the coastline closely. From records of seal surveys carried out years before, I knew that there had been large herds at Cape Dolphin, the northern tip of East Falkland; but, though the cape was clearly visible, only a few seal could be seen. According to the crew and master of the *Philomel*, a dearth of seal had been noted for several years; and, before the voyage was completed, I had found that many other colonies that had once been quite large were similarly depleted. I decided to go into the matter further and started to make notes on what I saw.

From Cape Dolphin, we crossed the Falkland Sound and entered the narrow Tamar Pass between West Falkland and the long, narrow island of Pebble. Within this area is a mass of smaller islands. I noticed that few of these were covered with tussac grass, which presumably had been eaten out years before by sheep. Later we passed Keppel and Saunders islands, the latter having been the site of the first British settlement, in 1763. Again, there was no tussac, though early descriptions of this island indicate that there was once a thick belt of it around the coast. Instead, there are now large areas of fern, diddle-dee (a very common dwarf shrub of the Falklands), fachine bush and fine grasslands. Sealers, who early on burnt much of the original vegetation, and sheep and cattle had greatly changed the nature of the island's flora.

Calling briefly at Carcass Island, we passed on to West Point; and from there, in the failing evening light, I could just make out the Jason group stretching away into the distance. At West Point I was to wait a few days for the arrival of the *Penelope*, which would be taking me out to the Jasons. The boat had been held up, but I was grateful for the delay as it gave me a chance to see how a small settlement operated and to discuss with Roddy Napier some of the things I had seen on the voyage out.

West Point is a sheep farm, but the tussac grass round the coast has been preserved. It is fenced in, and the sheep are allowed into it only during winter. In the spring, the tussac is cleared of sheep and left to the large colonies of Magellan penguins, for which it provides invaluable protection during the breeding season. The birds' excreta ensure that the tussac flourishes, and this in turn ensures that there is ample winter feed for the sheep. So well balanced in this system, which was then quite novel to me, that I was amazed that only two or three farms operated it. Later I discovered that the majority of farms had destroyed their tussac through overgrazing, and were not now prepared to go to the cost of replacing it. In the case of West Point, Roddy's father had had the foresight to preserve the grass and had encouraged his son to continue the system.

My arrival at West Point happened to coincide with a bird-banding programme that Roddy had been asked to carry out for the United States Antarctic Research Programme. On the cliffs on the seaward side of the island were several colonies of black-browed albatross and it was on these that the banding was to be carried out. One of the main colonies was on the seaward slopes of Mount Misery, the highest point on the island, rising to over a thousand feet above sea level. To get to the rookeries we first had to make the

Golden Grebe

Rolland's or Golden grebe (*Podiceps Rolland*), a race confined to the Falkland Islands. Although more commonly frequenting fresh water ponds and streams, where it nests and feeds, it is equally adapted to the Islands' tidal creeks and coastal waters.

strenuous climb to the top of the mountain, from which there is a breathtaking view over the west Falklands, with the sharply pointed mountains of Steeple Jason just visible to the north-west, and New Island visible to the south-west. In the immediate foreground are cliffs, which drop down to the sea over 800 feet below. Every few hundred yards along these cliffs are water-worn ravines in the vicinity of which the ground is wet and covered with tussac and other grasses. Dotted about these areas were the albatross youngsters, each sitting on top of a nest composed of mud, clay and pieces of vegetation. As we approached these grey downy young, with their ridiculously large feet and bills, they shuffled round on the top of their pedestal-like nests to face us, at the same time making a clapping sound with their bills. This was a defence mechanism coming into operation, for as soon as one came within holding distance of a young bird it would disgorge its stomach contents. Because of this it was necessary to wear oil skins, which made the work of banding particularly hot and difficult. The shallow ravines on these cliffs often act as a sun trap, making oil skins almost unbearable; but, much as we sweated, this was decidedly better than being drenched in oil, half-digested fish, octopods and krill.

After repeated delays, the *Penelope* eventually arrived; and, following one unsuccessful attempt to reach the islands, we again headed out to sea. The Jasons are a chain of islands that run out from West Falkland and protrude into the Falkland Current, which sweeps up from Antarctica, past the archipelago, and on to the area of the Rio de la Plata. The Jasons act as a baffle to this current, which, as it squeezes between the islands and over the many underwater ridges, forms tide rips, which, depending on the wind and tidal currents, can boil the sea into a fury. Thus, though the weather was fine, we were in stormy waters, and had to fight to make headway against the tides.

I was astounded by the vast numbers of sea birds that frequented these disturbed waters; everywhere we looked were petrels, albatross, prions, terns and gulls. Fur seal, too, were there in abundance: as we passed South and Elephant Jason, large groups of them could be seen leaping in and out of the water like porpoises. Later a whale surfaced very close to our bows, then slid out of sight. Although I was not to know it at the time, I was not to see another whale for eleven years! Now and again the white foaming water appeared pink in colour, and when the opportunity presented itself a bucket was put over the side and its contents hauled in. Darting about the water were dozens of red shrimp-like creatures—the krill, or, more properly, Euphausians, that form the basic food of all the baleen whales and of many species of birds and seal. Clearly, turbulence of the water was bringing these creatures to the surface, and it was this that was attracting the countless birds and seal.

Taking the shortest course to Grand and Steeple Jason, we sailed to the south of the island chain, which, however, is the side on which the tides are most turbulent. As we were to put in on the north side of Grand Jason, we changed course as we came up to the island, and passed through the island chain into a sea that was as calm as the sea on the southern side had been rough. The change was dramatic and our bodies took some time to get used to it after the continual movement to which they had been subjected for four or five hours previously. A few days later I stood on the top of Grand Jason looking back over the route we followed, and could see on the water's surface a distinct line marking where the underwater reefs intercepted the current, causing the strong tide rips that we had come through. Sometimes, when the wind is favourable, the sea here is much calmer; and on her journey back the *Penelope* had a much easier passage than she had had on the voyage out.

Although Grand and Steeple Jason lie close to each other, they are very different in appearance. Whereas Grand Jason is dominated by a large dome-shaped mountain, the main characteristic of Steeple is a range of sharply pointed hills, forming a backbone to the island. So sharp is the main ridge that in some places it is possible to straddle it and obtain a view down both sides. On the southern side of both islands the ground runs steeply from the mountains to the sea, forming impressive cliffs; but to the north the land shelves more gently and there are wide, fairly level plains, where I saw my first big colonies of penguins. Some 15,000 Gentoo penguins nested in these areas, but the largest bird colonies were on the south side of the islands.

There I found vast mixed colonies of black-browed albatross and rockhopper penguins, with smaller groups of king cormorants. Tens of thousands of birds were packed close together. It amazed me that so little was known about these colonies—indeed, that so few even knew of their existence.

While I already knew that the surrounding seas were rich in marine life, it was not until a few days after my arrival in the islands that I realised just how abundant those riches were and how important they were to the birds nesting in the group. From a vantage point on Grand Jason, I saw, about ten miles to the north, what at first appeared to be a low-lying island covered with nesting birds. Its position puzzled me, for I could not remember noting such an island on the map. On checking with binoculars, I witnessed a sight that I have yet to see equalled: the island was in fact a mass of birds spread over the surface of the sea, and obviously feeding off some huge food field. Although many species must have been present, the birds visible were albatross. Two days later this floating "island" of feeding birds had moved within a mile and a half of Grand Jason, and, though now much smaller, was some two or three miles long and about a hundred yards wide.

I had expected that the islands would contain large numbers of Johnny Rooks, which by some accounts were there in hundreds and were a pest to the sheep. However, on Grand Jason the highest count I made was fifty-two, these being mainly immature birds. To me these birds of prey were fascinating, particularly for their inquisitive nature and unusual and bold habits, which, I decided, had a lot to do with why farmers disliked them. If, say, a small piece of camera equipment were left unattended, it would not be long before one of these birds would descend to inspect and, perhaps, carry off the object, gripped in incredibly strong talons. Just how powerful these talons are I discovered when I made my first attempts at banding some of these birds. Rarely do they strike with their beak while being held, but they do lunge out with their talons and grip fingers or hand as in a vice. Often it is only with somebody else's help that the talons can be prised open.

The method used for catching Johnny Rooks, on whose beaks farmers paid a bounty, took advantage of the birds' natural curiosity and powerful grip. A bird caught with a baited noose would be fastened on its back in such a way as to enable it to strike with its talons. Other Johnny Rooks would then come to inspect the victim, only to be grasped by the talons of the pinioned bird and held until they also were taken and pinioned. In this way dozens of birds could be caught with little effort.

Although Mr Monk, the manager of Steeple and Grand Jason, had told me that personally he thought the Johnny Rooks did little damage to the sheep, clearly many thought otherwise and a lot of birds were being killed. Yet there appeared to be little evidence for the accusations made against the bird, and there was plenty of evidence that any damage the bird did do was largely attributable to the systems of sheep farming in general use. On Grand Jason and Steeple, as on many other unsettled islands, the sheep were left to fend for themselves, and were rarely visited more than once a year. On this annual visit, the sheep were gathered, sheared and dipped, and the lambs marked and operated upon. As there was no shepherding, it was impossible to tell what befell the sheep between one visit and the next, and yet the birds were being blamed for poor lambing. However, because there was no control over the rams, lambing was early, and it is likely that bad weather was responsible for the death of many newborn lambs. Further, when we visited Steeple and Grand Jason, many of the lambs were six months old or more; and, thus, ear-marking, tailing and castrating, which when performed fairly soon after birth are simple and bloodless operations, were left so late that the animals were leaving the pens covered in blood. As a result, many were weak and shocked, and predators were encouraged.

The same system of sheep farming had resulted in the destruction of tussac grass stands, mainly through overgrazing, and had left barren ground where once the grass had flourished and given shelter to birds, seal and sheep. Recently abandoned petrel and shearwater burrows provided tragic proof that this system of stocking islands with free-roaming sheep was not only depriving the sheep industry of valuable vegetation, but also destroying the habitats of species that relied on such cover for their existence. I could see no excuse for this practice, especially as there were proven methods of preserving this grass for the benefit of sheep and wildlife alike.

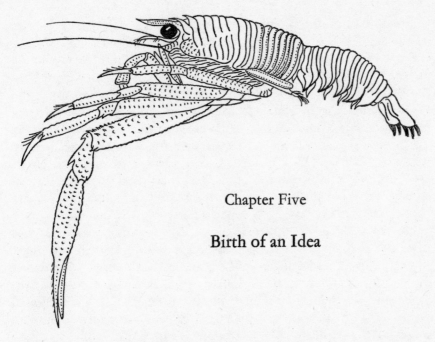

Chapter Five

Birth of an Idea

My first visit to the Jason group and other islands of the far west convinced me that these remote areas held the key to the survival of much of the Falklands' wildlife. Most of the large islands had been farmed for many years, and as a result habitats had disappeared or changed and a lot of animal and bird life had vanished from the islands. Clearly, tussac grass was the most important habitat, and little of this remained except on the smaller, more isolated islands, which therefore needed to be conserved if bird and animal populations were not to be further depleted. Admittedly, some species appeared not to have been greatly affected by the disappearance of tussac, as the survival of vast colonies of penguins and albatross on Steeple and Grand Jason showed; but many species had gone and it was by no means certain that those that were left would stay if the trend continued.

I became concerned about the other islands in the Jason group. These were owned by the Crown, but there was nothing to stop their being rented out for sheep grazing. At that time wool prices were low, so there was little interest in stocking these islands with sheep; but, if wool prices soared, someone would be bound to come up with a scheme for stocking the islands, and it would only be a matter of time before they were ruined.

Shortly before my trip to Steeple and Grand Jason, a new Colonial

Secretary had been appointed, and he, knowing my interest in seal, had asked if I would make out a report on the animals I saw during the trip. On my return I received a letter asking me about my findings and inquiring for my views on the possibility of exploiting the islands' fur seal and on the suitability of the Jasons for sheep grazing. Suddenly it appeared that my fears were justified. In my report I stressed that the seal herds in some areas appeared to have diminished considerably, and I expressed my views on the need to retain the Jason Islands as some sort of reserve for wildlife. However, my case was hampered by the fact that I had no experience of setting up such reserves; that I had seen what could eventually happen was unfortunately no support for my proposals.

One of the main supporters of my conservation proposals was Roddy Napier, who as a sheep farmer was able to offer me much valuable advice and guidance. We combined our efforts, and, aided by useful suggestions and assistance from Robin Woods, a meteorologist also interested in conservation, forwarded to the Colonial Secretary a further series of proposals dealing with wildlife and its preservation. Although we heard that consideration would be given to making Kidney Island a reserve, and that the laws governing the protection of certain birds would be reviewed, our attempts bore little fruit. This was frustrating, for the suggestions we had made were for simple precautions that could easily have been adopted.

In June 1962 I made my first contact with the International Union for Conservation of Nature (IUCN). The Secretary-General, Sir Hugh Elliott, wrote to me in concern about the establishment of the fur farm in the Falklands, and in my reply to him I mentioned my keen interest in the islands' wildlife and its conservation. This was the beginning of a long association with Sir Hugh, and I was to be constantly encouraged and guided by him in matters concerning the islands' wildlife.

By January 1963 I had gathered a lot more information on islands that I considered would make suitable reserves. One thing was obvious: only islands that were not used by the sheep industry and were too isolated or difficult to work could be considered. In January I wrote for advice to Sir Hugh Elliott, explaining that I was preparing to forward a plan to the Falkland Islands Government recommending that certain islands be designated wildlife reserves. I hoped that the IUCN might be able to undertake their protection. Later I learned from Sir Hugh that the IUCN could not do this and that it was up to the Falkland Islands Government to frame its own protective legislation. I submitted my proposals to the Government, but obtained no positive results. Perhaps, given my lack of success with earlier and less far-reaching proposals, the scheme was too ambitious.

In May I was due leave in England, and, rather than travel there direct, I arranged to go by way of Argentina, Canada, the United States and Iceland. I had discovered that there were a number of fur farms in the province of Buenos Aires, Argentina, and on visiting the area I obtained some valuable information. In North America I renewed contact with Dr Murphy, and through him met the ornithologists Dr Dean Amadon, Tom Gilliard and Dr Eizerman, all of whom gave me useful advice and encouragement.

Moving on to Iceland, I met Dr Finnur Gudmundsson, who was in charge of the Natural History Museum at Reykjavik. He explained to me some of the conservation problems experienced in Iceland, and, since some of these were similar to the Falklands' conservation problems, the value of this meeting is obvious.

On reaching London I met Sir Hugh Elliott for the first time and discussed further the problems I had already written to him about. In particular, I told him of my despondency at not having made any real progress in advancing the cause of conservation in the Falklands, and said that the backing of some respected body was needed in order to convice the islands' legislature that measures to conserve our wildlife were required urgently if it was not to be too late.

Back in the Falklands, I again raised the question of conservation with the Governor, Sir Edwin Arrowsmith, who I felt was sympathetic towards some forms of preservation. In a letter to Sir Hugh I explained that the Governor had been interested in my proposals and that, while he felt that it might be difficult to introduce any far-reaching conservation measures, he had encouraged me to continue my work and to try to have some of the smaller islands set aside as reserves. Soon after, I had heard that the Government was reviewing the possibility of designating Kidney and Cochon islands as reserves, and I told Sir Hugh of this promising development. He wrote back commenting on this news and told me that he hoped that Ambassador Philip Kingsland Crowe, a retired American diplomat, would shortly visit the Falklands on behalf of the World Wildlife Fund (WWF) and IUCN, to encourage the Falkland Government to take measures to conserve the islands' wildlife and natural resources. Later I learnt that the Government had received a personal letter from the Chairman of the WWF, HRH Prince Philip, mentioning the proposed visit by Ambassador Crowe. The scene was set for the first major step towards conservation.

Before my trip to England the chance had arisen for me to obtain a boat. She was the ten-ton cutter *Gleam*. When I first saw her, she was on the Stanley slipway awaiting overhaul, having suffered damage in a heavy sea, and she looked a sorry sight. News reached me that she was up for sale, as her false keel was infested with marine worm; but on closer inspection it turned out that she was not as badly infested as had been thought. Accordingly I bought her, and, though the repair of her keel raised some awkward technical problems, these were overcome. Once she was sound I used her mainly for travelling about the north-east coast of East Falkland; and for this she proved invaluable.

Although the amount of work on the farm had increased, I now had assistance and was more easily able to find time for exploration and to take the leave due to me. With the problem of sea transport overcome, it was possible for me to leave Stanley late in the evening or very early in the morning, carry out observations, and return to continue with the farm work in the normal way. By this means I was able to complete surveys of all islands and areas within a day's sailing of Stanley, and to gather a lot of information on seal and bird life.

One island that was too far away to be visited on these short excursions, but that I found of special interest, was Beauchêne Island. This is the most remote island in the archipelago, lying some forty miles off the south-east corner of East Falkland. Until two years previously, when the Royal Navy's ice patrol vessel *Protector* had briefly visited it, no one had landed on Beauchêne since 1919, when sealers last worked the island. From the crew of *Protector* I had obtained a little information on the island, and this had convinced me that Beauchêne should be surveyed as a potential wildlife reserve. Clearly, because of its remoteness it was of no use to the sheep farming industry, and thus was an obvious candidate for conservation.

On 2 December 1963, accompanied by two members of the crew of *Protector*, I made my first visit to Beauchêne Island. Within ten minutes of landing, I had seen enough to convince me that the island was of immense value and should become a reserve; but, though I hastened to make my feelings known, and a brief note appeared in *The Guardian* stating that it was thought that Beauchêne would make an excellent wildlife reserve, it was over ten years before the island obtained the protection that it deserved.

In March 1964 Ambassador Crowe arrived for his tour of the Falklands and at the same time I submitted a memorandum on conservation to the Government. Besides outlining a plan, this memorandum listed all the islands that I felt were of special value. Kingsland Crowe's visit came rather late in the season and I was disappointed that he was not able to see the islands at their best. On 17 March, in the most miserable conditions, I took the Crowes out to Kidney Island in the hope of showing them something of a tussac island. I do not think there is anything more uncomfortable than pushing through high tussac when it is raining, and though we were wearing oilskins we were soon soaked. Fortunately the Ambassador saw the humorous side of the situation, exclaiming, "If tussac grass is what conservation is in aid of, to hell with conservation, at least when it's raining!"

All the same, Ambassador Crowe's visit was a success, and soon afterwards the Reserves and Sanctuaries Ordinance was passed. The part dealing with reserves was as I had hoped and provided that land designated a reserve would be strictly controlled and virtually closed. However, the legislation relating to sanctuaries came as a surprise, and dismayed me. Generally speaking, any land designated a sanctuary was protected against persons shooting or trapping, but it was not unlawful to stock the area with sheep, cattle or horses. This greatly reduced the practical value of the legislation, since it was not the man with a gun but stock grazing that was doing the real damage. Obviously, the Government, which in taking a new look at conservation had to take into account the needs of the sheep industry on which the colony relied for its existence, had decided on a compromise. I was afraid that many of the islands I had listed as potential reserves would be given sanctuary status, thus permitting their use by the sheep industry. Of course, it was possible that landowners would apply for sanctuary status to be given to land that was already stocked but that they wished to have extra protection. However, I felt that any landowner who wished to protect wildlife from being shot or trapped on his property would rely on his own system of protection anyway.

It was some months before the first reserves and sanctuaries were declared, and in the meantime local sheep farmers, concerned, no doubt, that they would lose potential grazing, applied for the lease of Kidney Island. Though I was fairly confident that, after all the recommendations that this island be made a reserve, the Government would not allow the lease, I was worried about a reversal and therefore continued to put forward reasons for protecting the island.

On 23 October 1964 Kidney and Cochon Islands were declared nature reserves, and on 30 December Low Island, (owned by West Point) and The Twins (formerly ownerless and now the property of Carcass) were declared sanctuaries! So, to my amazement, was Beauchêne, which in a letter to the Colonial Secretary the same month I had suggested was the foremost candidate for reserve status. However, late in November the Colonial Secretary replied that "Beauchêne Island belongs to the Crown and seems to protect itself. It is so remote that a technical declaration making it a nature reserve would have no practical effect and if anyone went there we might never know about the visit." I agreed with him on this last point, but argued that, without the "technical declaration", we could not even start to formulate ideas for its protection. One of the best protections is advertising to the world the existence of such a reserve. I was sure that if we did this, and began to instil the idea that this was a valuable, ecologically perfect island, the island would come to be recognised as such the world over, and we should avoid possible protection problems in the future.

Later I began to wonder if the decision to declare Beauchêne a sanctuary rather than a reserve had anything to do with the Falkland Islands Company's claim to the island. According to one of the company's directors, Bill Blake, the Royal Charter issued to the company in 1852 gave it the right to all islands to the south of Lafonia (on the mainland), a description that would cover Beauchêne Island even though it was not specifically mentioned. Owing to this and the island's fur seal colony, the company had laid claim to the island, but the claim had not been recognised and the seal herds had vanished, causing the company to lose interest.

Although I was then an employee of the company and understood its interests and concerns, I could not be happy that a company owning 46 per cent of the entire land surface of the Falkland Islands showed so little interest in the conservation of wildlife. It is significant that when, eventually, the company had half of one of its islands designated a sanctuary, wildlife was just beginning to attract increased commercial interest.

Towards the end of 1964 I was becoming concerned for my future in the Falklands. The time had come for an assessment of the fur farm's performance and future prospects, and if these were not good it was doubtful that the experiment would continue. We had worked hard at adapting the mink's breeding cycle to the southern hemisphere, at trying to overcome the problems associated with feeding the mink mutton rather than red meat, and at balancing the mink's need for sunlight with its need for protection from the incessant winds. However, we had had only partial success with the climatic and dietary problems, and were having to feed the mink more imported foods than was economically viable for the success of the project. I remained hopeful of success, but it had begun to seem that it was not going to be attained.

Owing to my interest in wildlife, the farm had become rather like a small zoo. I had a collection of upland geese, which bred happily in captivity; several species of duck wandered around; and I had a number of Johnny Rooks and other birds of prey. Much to the delight of Shona and Sharron, who were now old enough to appreciate such things, I had two young fur seal, which I had reared from the age of a few weeks. They became incredibly tame and would follow me around like dogs, causing havoc when they managed to slip into the kitchen! They were continually active, showing the most amazing agility. Using much the same technique as a rock-climber uses to back up a "chimney" or cleft in a rockface, they would often work their way between two pipes to the top of our two-storey house and sit at the top of the pipes, apparently quite at ease. On seeing me they would utter their odd-sounding bark and without hesitation release themselves from their precarious position and slide backwards the eighteen or twenty feet down to the ground! I hoped to get them to take to the wild again while still allowing me to approach them. These hopes were dashed when at about the age of six months they caught some form of enteritis, which within two days proved fatal.

In November 1964 the Wild Animals and Birds Protection Ordinance was brought up to date. This in its old form had provided for the protection of an extensive list of species; but, as there were many that were not listed, Robin Woods had suggested that it would be better if the Ordinance instead listed unprotected species, so ensuring wider coverage and making it unnecessary to consider all the birds that might happen to fly over from the South American continent. During the final stages in the preparation of the Ordinance, I was consulted, and was shocked to see that, in addition to the islands' two species of geese, the turkey vulture and the carancho (but, fortunately, not the Johnny Rook), the cormorant, skua, Dominican gull and thin-billed prion were listed as birds that might be killed at any time. The geese, birds of prey and perhaps the Dominican gull were not really any surprise, but I certainly had not expected to find the other species on the list. On inquiry, I found that the cormorant was listed because it was feared that it would deplete recently introduced stocks of brown trout (ridiculous, but an indication of the type of attitude we were up against), and that the skua was listed for its habit of diving on shepherds and its predation of penguin rookeries. I pointed out that these habits of the skua are very natural and that the latter is of importance to the penguins themselves; but my efforts to have the bird removed from the list were in vain.

The thin-billed prion (a species of petrel) also remained on the list. It had been listed because the owners of the island on which it had its main breeding grounds had complained of the bird's burrows. The species was not uncommon but I felt strongly that it was wrong that the bird should be listed for the benefit of a single farm. I argued that, if this farm's complaint were justified, a special licence should be issued that could be withdrawn if it were found that the bird were being endangered. However, though I raised the matter several times, I had no success, and certainly did not foresee that some years later I would become responsible for this bird's survival on that very island.

Early in 1965 I again submitted proposals for the protection of the Jason group and Bird Island. I explained that if these islands were designated reserves, just about every species breeding in the Falklands would enjoy some measure of protection. Above all, I was anxious to persuade the Government to give reserve status to the Crown-owned islands in the Jason group—South Jason, Elephant Jason, Flat Jason, South and North Fur, The Fridays, and East and West Cay. This would mean that the entire group, excepting the privately owned islands of Steeple and Grand Jason, would be protected. I hoped that if this proposal were accepted it would eventually be possible to extend the reserve to include the sea area around the group.

Though I obtained no positive answer to these proposals, I refused to be discouraged and continued to offer suggestions and press for action. Probably my determination caused me to overstep the bounds of correct protocol, but I was worried that, as we appeared to be making progress in one direction, we were sliding backwards in another. It was rumoured that on New Island large numbers of Gentoo penguins were being killed for the damage they were supposedly doing to the pastures there; and it was even suggested that permission had been given for this. I was naturally concerned for the fate of the penguins, but my main worry was that, while everything appeared to confirm these rumours, the authorities were doing nothing to check on what was happening. Many years later I found ample evidence that the rumours had been largely true, but by then the damage had been done.

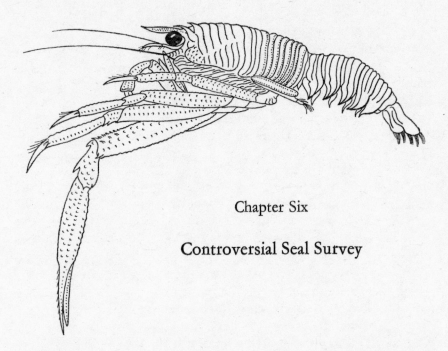

Chapter Six

Controversial Seal Survey

It had become apparent that something was wrong with the sealion herds in the Falklands, numbers having decreased dramatically since the census taken by Dr Hamilton in the 1930s. I had repeatedly pointed this out to the Government, but either my reports were doubted or it was thought that they gave little cause for concern. Now it seemed that a new sealing licence was to be issued, with what results it was horrifying to contemplate.

Since my visit to Beauchêne Island in December 1963 I had also become concerned about the fur seal. For many years Beauchêne had been reputed to be one of the principal breeding grounds of fur seal in the Falklands, though nobody had actually been there to see if it was. Dr R. H. Laws, who, in carrying out his survey in 1951, had been unable to visit Beauchêne, had been convinced by local hearsay that these breeding grounds still existed, and had credited them with a large proportion of the Falkland fur seal population. I too was convinced by what I heard, but when I visited the island I saw not one fur seal. I was prepared to accept that a small herd might yet be found hidden away under the cliffs, but certainly there was no major colony on the island. This was serious, for if, in the mistaken belief that there were vast herds on the island, a licence to take fur seal were at some time issued, the effect on the total Falkland population would probably be disastrous.

The whole matter came to a head when Dr Martin Holdgate, then in charge of the BAS biology unit, called in at the islands on his way south. I had spoken to him earlier about the apparent decrease in the number of sealions and he had shown a great deal of interest. Although he could not spend more than a few days in Stanley, I knew it was likely that the Government would approach him on the question. Just before Dr Holdgate left Stanley on 25 November 1963, I was told by him it had been decided to issue a sealing licence.

I was horrified at this and found it incredible that, whatever was thought of my own reports, no effort was being made to check the herds first. I knew my reports were hard to accept, for I was suggesting that since the 1930s, when Hamilton (in reports dated 1934 and 1939) had estimated the total number of sealion in the Falklands at 380,000, of which 80,000 were pups, the sealion population had fallen by 70–80 per cent. The attitude the Government took to my reports is typified by the reply I received from a Council member whom I asked about the wisdom of trusting to the Hamilton figures without making any effort to check whether they remained valid. He argued, "Surely the herds would have increased more like twenty times as the survey was done more than twenty years ago". The known fact that I had travelled round the islands observing and checking on seal herds was apparently seen as no reason to expect that I knew better than those who had never taken the trouble to look closely at even one seal herd. Instead my reports were written off as those of a wildlife crank.

In July I had spoken to the Officer Administrating about my fears that sealion would, if a licence were issued, be taken from Kidney and Cochon Islands, which were viewed as potential reserves (declared in October). In a letter the same month I had pointed out the close connection between the Kidney Island herd and the breeding grounds on Top and Bottom Islands, which lie close to Kidney. I suspected that, if animals were taken from these two islands, the herd on Kidney would suffer.

Either my letter was not heeded or it came too late, for on 15 August I wrote to Dr Holdgate reporting that sealing had commenced, with animals being taken from Top and Bottom Islands. I explained, as I had to the Colonial Secretary, that there were very few seal in the area of Stanley and that a valuable herd was now being badly depleted. I also stated my intention to prove that the herds had decreased drastically since Hamilton's survey. I wrote, "I am continually making inquiries about the position of seal colonies

The author examines one of the new prions he found on Beauchêne Island.

The vast colony of Black-browed albatross and Rockhopper penguin on Beauchêne Island. They were so closely knit that it was impossible to walk without treading on birds, nests or eggs.

(*above*) One of the colonies on Steeple Jason Island. The sister island Grand Jason is in the background. The two are now important private reserves. (*below*) A view in the opposite direction from Steeple Jason looking out over Grand Jason. In the background (top right) are Elephant and South Jason Islands.

(*above*) During gales on Beauchêne Island the very ground seemed to shake with the crash of great breakers. (*below*) The main colony of King penguins at Volunteer point. They nested together with a group of Gentoo penguins on a shoulder of land beside the sheltered lagoon.

A Johnny Rook, an endangered species. The Falklands may be one of their last breeding grounds.

and numbers, and time and time again I am getting the same answer: the colony has disappeared, or there are only a few compared to what there were ten years ago."

Ambassador Crowe's visit to the Falklands in March had led to a recommendation that I receive a small WWF grant to use in making a general survey of wildlife. I now decided that it should be used in making intensive surveys of the islands' seal herds. Though the grant had yet to be confirmed, I was anxious to start organising; and, as soon as I had obtained the Colonial Secretary's permission to carry out the survey, I started to make plans.

The only satisfactory way of checking the herds was by aerial survey. During my travels I had built up a fairly accurate map of the location of all the important seal colonies and had visited quite a large number to obtain ground counts. In some cases I had been able to check the reliability of aerial photography relative to that of ground counts, and was satisfied that the aerial method was better. As I intended basing total population figures on the number of pups counted, timing was very important and the census had to be carried out at a period when all pupping had finished and when the pups were forming "pods" or small groups. I had calculated that the best period would be mid January.

By early January 1965 we were ready for the survey. To overcome certain practical difficulties in making observations from the Beaver float plane, the Air Service had removed one of the main cabin windows in the aircraft and fitted a windshield, so that an observer had a clear view for taking aerial shots. Owing to unfavourable weather conditions, our start was delayed; and, while we were waiting, the BAS research ship *John Biscoe* arrived in Stanley. On board was a Government sealing officer, Bill Vaughan from South Georgia. He had made an unscheduled arrival in Stanley because of bad weather, which prevented his landing on South Georgia. We had never met or corresponded before, but became acquainted through our mutual interest in seal. Before long I was explaining my plans for the survey, and he, though he told me he had never seen a sealion before, said he would be pleased to help during his enforced stay in the Falklands. As he was a seal biologist this seemed excellent, and I agreed that any report that emerged from the survey and that he was prepared to assist me in writing up could be published as a joint paper.

The survey started on 20 January, when we covered the south and north coasts of East Falkland. Unfavourable conditions then delayed progress until 2 February, when most of the Jason group was surveyed. The final survey was made on 5 March, when some of the more remote regions were covered. By this time we had flown over 1,500 miles, covering all those areas surveyed by Dr Hamilton, plus a large number of others. We had had no difficulty in counting the seal, but this, alas, was because there were so few! Three of us had taken part in the survey, and the procedure had been for each of us to make counts and photograph each colony. Afterwards the figures were compared, and were checked against the aerial photographs and, where appropriate, the ground counts that I had made earlier.

Two preliminary reports were drawn up. The first compared Dr Hamilton's 1937 figures for some of the Jason group with our counts for the same area. Whereas Dr Hamilton had counted 29,600 sealion pups in the area, we had counted only 1,230—a much more severe drop than I had anticipated; and it became clear that I had to get out a full report as quickly as possible. As I considered it important that the report should contain some background history, and as Bill Vaughan had better facilities for seeing to the preparation of the final report, it was agreed that all the information be taken to England and compiled into one report. Bill Vaughan left for England soon after completion of the survey, and I carried out further surveys, in order to check the reliability of the original counts.

In mid December 1965 I received a note from Dr Martin Holdgate enclosing a copy of the completed survey report, which now bore the title "An Aerial Survey of the Sea Lion Stocks in the Falkland Islands, by William Vaughan B.Sc. and Ian J. Strange". The final results were as expected, the number of sealions being dramatically smaller than in the 1930s, when Dr Hamilton had estimated the total population (all age groups) at 380,000. Our highest figure for the total population was 30,000. Figures were also given for the total fur seal population, which we calculated at no more than 14,000. Oddly enough, Dr Laws had obtained the same figure for the colonies that he had visited in 1951, but his belief that there was a large colony on Beauchêne Island had forced his overall total higher. Our conclusion, then, was that the fur seal population had increased little, if at all, since 1951.

Now that I had the completed report, I was anxious to convey the information to the Colonial Secretary, Mr W. H. Thompson, so I immediately rang him to ask if he would be interested to see it. I was somewhat surprised to hear that he had already read it, and that he was not too pleased about it. Other than the drastic reduction in the sealion population, I could see nothing in the report to cause displeasure, and thus was anxious to have a second opinion. Accordingly, I showed the report to Mr A. G. Barton, who was not only my superior in the Falkland Islands Company but also a member of Executive Council; I had great respect for his judgement and felt that if anything in the report was detrimental to the Government he would inform me. In his reply, he said that he had found nothing critical of the Government, but that he thought the statement of the present sealion population rather "sweeping". Others echoed this opinion, even though the survey had been as thorough, if not more thorough, than any preceding it.

In discussing the report with the Colonial Secretary, I found that his concern had been over the wording of the final paragraph. This read,

The fact that the sealion resources of the Falklands have reached a dangerously low level has been established. The fact that they, together with the fur seals, could, if properly managed, become an important economic asset is obvious. If these resources are to be neglected, and perhaps slaughtered unlawfully in consequence, the islands will lose a potential valuable source of income which would probably cost little to maintain.

Hard words perhaps; but I was writing in the knowledge that a sealing licence had been issued and animals taken before anybody was certain that the herds could support a sealing venture. I said that I was prepared to rephrase this paragraph before publishing the report—not realising that I should not be allowed to do so.

The report, I was told, could not be released for publication as it was a Government one! This view was based on the fact that Bill Vaughan was a Government employee and had received a Government salary while the report was being written up. I was stunned. After all, the survey had been my idea, had been back by my own, independent investigations, and had been paid for by a WWF grant and more than £150 of my own money. This, I was told, did not matter, and nor did the fact that Vaughan's participation in the survey had been the result of pure coincidence and at my invitation. One of the most unpleasant features of my battle to have my claims recognised was that on 4 March 1966, three months after the report

had been finalised, the following circular was sent out from the
Secretariat to all farm managers:

> Various world authorities on wild life are for ever asking us how
> many seal we have in the Falkland Islands. The only figures
> available to us are those produced by Dr Hamilton before the
> last war, and the indication is that his figures no longer stand up
> to inspection. I do not want to put you to any trouble but I am
> asking your co-operation in identifying seal rookeries together
> with some estimate of their respective seal populations.
>
> It would be a help when your employees are riding around if
> they could be asked to note seal rookeries and give some estimate
> of the population. If you could drop me a very brief note as and
> when the information is obtained we can, perhaps, over the next
> year or so build up some form of adequate picture. I do not ask
> you to organise any particular search for seal rookeries.
>
> Your help will be much appreciated.

The report was never published, though two years later I was
informed I could use it, perhaps rewriting it under my name. By this
time it was out of date and required another back-up survey to give
it value—an undertaking that was financially beyond my means.
However, though the report was never published, the information
was used and, I believe, did a lot to change the Government's view
on sealing. Ironically, sealing stopped soon after the report was
finished, simply because there were too few seal for the venture to
be economically viable: though a licence to take 1,500 skins had
been issued, only 350 were shipped away.

On Christmas Eve 1965 I learned that the mink farm would have to
be closed down and that I would be losing my job. I was half
expecting this, for although the experiment had worked it was
obvious that the farm would not be a commercial success. I was
sorry, as a lot of work had gone into the scheme; but at the same
time I realised that the establishment of a fur farm in the islands
represented a very real danger to wildlife, in whose conservation I
was above all interested.

Now that I knew I would be losing my job, I started to look for
ways in which I might stay in the Falklands and continue my work
on conservation. Through Martin Holdgate, Sir Hugh Elliot of the

IUCN Liaison Office had received a copy of the sealion census and of a report on Beauchêne Island that I had written. In January 1966 he wrote to me about these and also to say that he had had a long discussion with Martin about my wish to stay in the islands. He was sorry to say that neither of them could see any solution to the problem, unless I could somehow link my work with the re-establishment of a sealing industry.

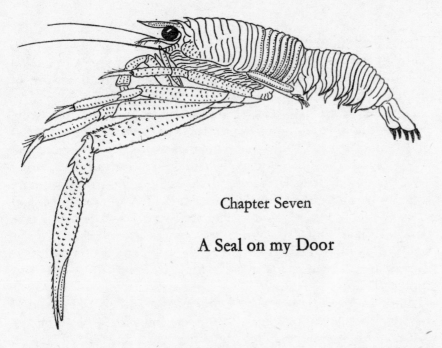

Chapter Seven

A Seal on my Door

Although I had given a great deal of attention to sealion, I was particularly fascinated by fur seal. Unfortunately, their breeding sites were well chosen, and the five or six main colonies in the Falklands were situated in the most inaccessible spots. The only one that lay within easy reach of Stanley was that on Volunteer Rocks, about twelve miles away; but, though the rocks lie only a few hundred yards off the coast of East Falkland, their formidable nature and exposure to wind and sea had made them a self-protecting home for the seal that lived there.

Little was known about the Falkland species of fur seal, and the physical difficulties of obtaining information about them had militated against attempts to carry out a systematic study. Several times I had sailed past or flown over Volunteer Rocks, and once had attempted to land there, though unsuccessfully. Many were of the opinion that the dangers were too great for a landing to be feasible; but, as there were records that sealers had worked and, apparently, lived there for short periods, it seemed that a landing was possible. In 1961 I asked the Government if some aerial photographs could be taken of the rocks, so that their seal population could be estimated; but when photographs were taken they revealed other important information as well.

Clearly visible on the photographs was a small gulch with a steep boulder beach that is not visible from the sea. Almost certainly this was where the sealers had landed. Evidence of occupation also emerged, for lying up against a large rock could be seen a collection of timbers, which had obviously been placed there as a form of shelter.

Now that I had *Gleam*, attempts at landing on the rock were possible, but it was not until the winter of 1965 that the first successful landing was made. We treated the rocks with all due respect, and it was a long while before we sufficiently overcame our fears. However, once that had been done and we had made our first landing, landings became quite frequent and were made both in summer and in winter. A voyage from Stanley to the rocks would generally take two and a half hours, so, taking into account the return journey as well, the amount of time left for study was not great. I therefore decided to try living on the rocks for a while, as the sealers had apparently done.

A few weeks after the first landing, I and four others were ferrying ashore rather precarious loads of timber, and after a busy four or five hours a structure resembling a hut had been erected. I now began planning to spend a few nights living among the fur seal, though most of my friends thought the idea madness. We had been told numerous times that during bad weather the sea washed right over the rocks; but, though I had discovered kelp quite high up, I was sure that a large area remained clear of water. Spray would certainly go right over, but as the hut was reasonably watertight I saw no problems. Of course, there was a danger that I would be marooned for some time if the swell prevented my being reached, so I decided that it would be wisest to work on the island while HMS *Protector* and her helicopters were in the area.

Through my visit to Beauchêne Island, I had made friends with *Protector*'s skipper, Captain Sandford, who had shown a keen interest in assisting with surveys of wildlife. We had already planned to carry out by helicopter another seal survey of the north coast of East Falkland, and it was suggested that I combine this with a landing on Volunteer Rocks. Thus, on 21 January 1966, the survey was carried out and I was landed on the rocks by helicopter, with gear and stores for a few days' stay.

I had designed the hut in such a way that it nestled up against a large rock, which gave it extra protection on one side. Facing the main group of seal, I had a small observation window. Though the hut was very small (6 feet long by 4 feet wide, with a roof sloping from 5 feet to 3-4 feet above the ground), so was the island, and with some 2,000 seal in an area no more than an acre the place was somewhat crowded! Mainly because of this, I designed the hut to have a trap door in the roof rather than a side door, but this was a great mistake. One night it rained and water poured in round the edge of the trap; and one morning I had difficulty in getting out, because a seal was lying on the door!

Most of my previous visits to the rocks had been made during daylight hours, when the seal were comparatively restful, and I expected, rightly, that they would be most active at night. As evening approached, increasing numbers of seal would leave the rocks; and by nightfall there would be few left other than harem bulls and pups. At dawn the activity and noise would be quite fantastic as large numbers of females returned from the feeding grounds and called, in their shrill, high-pitched bark, for their pups. At first, it amazed me that individuals managed to locate each other; but later, when I listened to recordings of the din, I found that it was quite easy to pick out the calls of individual females and their pups, and even to follow a female's call as she made her way through the crowded rookery to her offspring.

On earlier visits, which had been brief, I had found the seal always suspicious of my movements, even though I took great care to move about quietly. However, after a couple of days of being with them on my own, I found, to my surprise, that even the bulls were beginning to accept me. No longer were they making charges at me, but, though watchful, remained lying in their territories. One day when it was calm and warm and I had half crawled my way into the centre of a mass of pups, who, probably because I now smelt like them, had taken little or no notice of me, I had stopped to note down my observations. No sooner was I settled than I had four or five pups lying over my outstretched legs. Later a female lay at my side while she suckled her pup, causing me to wonder how a sealer would feel if he found himself in that situation.

Some while afterwards I was told by an old sealer, Pop Porter, how he as a young man had crept with other sealers into the fur seal rookery on Elephant Jason. Without disturbing the seal, who lazed peacefully, the pups suckling at their mothers' teats, they had positioned themselves in a semi-circle round a large group and at a pre-arranged signal had fired with repeater rifles into the mass of seal. The scene, he told me, was horrible, with frightened pups rushing about the rocks spewing milk over the blood of their mothers. Now in his eighties, the old sealer thought the slaughter had been wrong.

Shortly after my sojourn on the rocks I returned to the colony with Shona, who was not then six years old. I was always keen to take the girls on my shorter excursions from Stanley, being sure that, young as they were, such experiences were important to them. Many people thought I really was mad to take a young child to a place like Volunteer Rocks, but by then I knew the place well enough to be sure that the risk was small and well worth the valuable experience and happy memories that Shona would be likely to derive from the trip.

I don't think any of the adults who made that trip will forget the delight on Shona's face at seeing the animals. As we rowed to the rocks from *Gleam*'s anchorage, we were surrounded by dozens of inquisitive fur seal. The water was so calm that we could watch the seal diving and then swimming on their backs beneath the boat. On the rock itself Shona was even more fascinated, and, although one harem bull made a number of half-hearted charges at us, she showed no fear. The purpose of the visit being to tag pups so that they could be identified later, I took the precaution of sitting Shona on the top of a rock out of harm's way, while we concentrated on the job. So engrossed did we become, that none of us noticed that the bull who had been taking an interest in us was now stretching and sniffing at Shona. How long he had been thus engaged I do not know, but as I turned I saw Shona patting him on the head and exclaiming what a nice dog he was. I had always believed that animals can sense whether a person shows fear of or threatens them, and here was an example. The child knew no fear of the creature, and the animal, sensing no threat, responded with trust.

Having clashed with the Falkland Government over the seal survey, I was surprised when on 10 May 1966 I heard that South Jason, Elephant Jason, North and South Fur, The Fridays, and East and West Cay had been declared sanctuaries by the Governor in Council, and that Flat Jason had been declared a reserve. At the same time, Middle Island (outside the Jason group), an island of nearly 400 acres, was declared a sanctuary. I was pleased that the Government appeared to be changing its attitude towards conservation, but was sadly disappointed that my recommendation that all these islands be made reserves had not been followed. None of them were of much use for sheep farming; yet all of them, with the exception of Flat Jason, had been made sanctuaries, which meant that they might still be used for grazing. This of course, was the very thing I was trying to prevent, and thus I was greatly disturbed when a few days later I learned that, for the first time in their history, South Jason (about 940 acres) and Elephant Jason (700 acres) were to be leased for sheep farming.

I immediately wrote to the recently-formed Natural Resources Committee, emphasising the great importance of these two islands, and that once sheep were placed on them their ecological value would be gone. I pointed out the difficulties of working such islands, and queried the profitability of such a move. Their very severe terrain was likely to prevent fencing even if (as was doubtful) it were the intention of the lessee to erect any.

Shortly afterwards I received a reply from the Governor saying that the leases would contain comprehensive safeguards. This I was sure meant only that shooting and trapping would not be allowed, and not that there would be attempts to protect the vegetation by fencing, or by limiting the number of sheep. A comparatively small number of sheep could, over a period of three or four years, do far more damage than any individuals armed with guns. Two of the finest islands, neither of which had been visited recently, were to be leased regardless of what was (or was not) known about their workability, vegetation, and so on—in short, their value to either farmer or conservation. As in the affair of the sealing licence, no one had bothered to find out the facts first, and needless damage would be caused.

In September I arranged to visit Carcass Island in order to record elephant seal pups. This island was one of the seal's main breeding grounds, and in spring the north-west end of the island would be covered with several hundred of these animals. Pupping generally commenced around the 12th, so I flew out to Carcass on the 9th in order to be there for the first pups. The flight by Beaver was the worst I had experienced, and when the small aircraft took off to return to Stanley I wondered if she would make it back.

The next two days were spent wandering in search of elephant seal pups. The task was made no easier by the wind, which made it impossible to hear the calls of pups, except within twenty yards. Even the angry roars of adult bulls fighting for territory were hardly audible at a distance of two or three hundred yards, though the sound normally travels miles. Bull seal weighing upwards of three tons each slapped into each other with a terrific noise, roaring and gasping for air, but I could record none of it; I could not even hold a microphone steady, let alone one attached to a reflector. After two days of recording little except wind howl, I had to admit defeat. By the 13th a full gale was blowing, with winds reaching 72 miles per hour. Winter was having her last hit at the islands before she allowed spring to come in.

Cecil and Kitty Bertrand, with whom I was staying, could not recall when a gale had lasted so long, and we all wondered what damage this one would cause. On the 15th I had a message from Stanley saying that *Gleam* had broken her moorings during the night and that, although she had gone ashore, by some miracle she had come to rest standing upright between two ridges of rock at the entrance to Stanley harbour. A few yards further to the north and she would have gone through the entrance and out to sea, or would have been driven ashore and smashed to pieces. She had been holed and flooded, but it was thought that she could be refloated at high tide and perhaps saved.

I immediately made arrangements to go back to Stanley, but the weather remained so bad that I could not do so until the 19th. Fortunately, when at last I was able to examine *Gleam*, I found that structurally she was still sound. A number of people had gone to her aid, but the person who assisted most was the very man who had taken out the controversial sealing licence. Though he must have thought me a thorn in his side, Chris Bundes was a seaman first and foremost, and, on seeing a vessel in trouble, had gone to her aid.

The damage to *Gleam* stopped my seal work, and, though I was able to beach her, do the repair work on the hull, and have her sea-worthy again by November, my studies of the seal colony on Volunteer Rocks suffered a damaging loss of continuity.

On 13 October 1966 my son Alistair Ian was born, and Irene, who had dearly wished for a son, was overjoyed. However, Irene and I were not greatly happy together; and, as she was anxious to return home to England, we agreed that it was best she did so. I should then stay on in the Falklands for a few months, attempting to complete some of my work on wildlife. After that, I should return to England, hoping eventually to find some research organisation that could put me back on the islands.

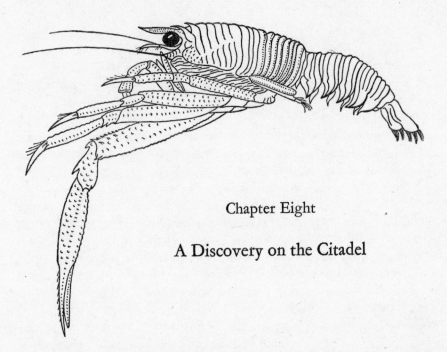

Chapter Eight

A Discovery on the Citadel

In December 1966, HMS *Protector* made a brief visit to Beauchêne Island to make further observations on its actual position; and, on the suggestion of Captain Sandford, I went along in order to prepare for an extended stay I was planning for the following month. On this short visit, and despite very poor weather conditions, we managed to land on the island by helicopter a hut and some of the equipment that I should need.

I planned to return in January for a stay of three weeks or more, depending on when *Protector* returned from patrols in the Antarctic. However, the Government made it a condition of my stay that I should not be on my own; and, though many of my friends were keen to go, it was difficult to find anyone who could spare the time. Finally Peter Westley, a teacher friend who had a holiday due, decided that he would come along. Peter's interest in birds was somewhat limited and this worried me a little, for I realised that Beauchêne could easily become oppressive to someone who was not absorbed in the study of its wildlife.

We set off in *Protector* on the night of 2 January, and by 6.30 a.m. the next day were in sight of the island. Beauchêne is about four kilometres long and a maximum of one kilometre wide, its orientation being north–south. The northern two-thirds of the island are roughly oblong in shape, with spectacular cliffs rising some 200 feet

above sea level on the eastern side. From there, the land slopes
gradually to the western coast, which is made up of boulder beaches
and shelving rocks. Towards the south the island is pinched in to
form a narrow waist, where the land surface is for the most part
covered with bare rock slabs and low-lying, reaching about 50 feet
above seal level on the east. The southernmost section of the island,
though no wider than the waist, is vastly more impressive, with
formidable cliffs rising about 250 feet from the sea. It has the
appearance of a fortress built of huge slabs of square-cut rock, and
because of this we later named it the Citadel.

As a heavy swell was running, we had to land and move in the
remainder of our equipment by helicopter. Once this had been done,
we were on our own on the most remote island of the Falkland
archipelago, an island that, prior to *Protector*'s visit there in 1962,
and my visits over the past few years, had not been visited or lived
on since October 1919. I had stopped overnight on the island in
December 1965, but nobody had lived there for any length of time
since sealers had last worked the island. On some rocks near our
camp site, some of these men had carved their names and the date of
their visits. Some of these inscriptions were accompanied by Roman
numerals, which I took to mean the number of sealskins taken.

Shortly after we had landed, rain began to threaten, so we pitched
one of our two tents and stowed away our food supplies and equipment. We planned to use the tents for sleeping and the hut, once it
had been erected, for cooking and storage. As soon as we had
finished stowing our supplies, we started assembling the hut, which
we placed in a shallow hollow that offered protection against all
winds except those from the east. By 10.30 p.m. and despite our
having several times been interrupted by rain, the hut was ready.

I decided to name the island's landmarks. The first I named was
the bay by which the hut stood and where the sealers' inscriptions
were. This I called Blinn's Bay, after "W. Blinn 1834", the oldest
inscription I had found. The hut Pete and I named after Captain
Sandford, who had been responsible for getting both us and the hut
to the island.

Our camp was hidden from the western shore by a gently rising
shoulder of land thickly covered in tussac grass. Coming from this
western shore was the low murmur of what sounded like surf. I had
heard the sound before and knew what it was; but, as Pete was
puzzled and had not yet seen the western side of the island, I
decided to show rather than tell him the cause of the noise.

The tussac was particularly luxuriant, much of it being over nine feet high; and, as a result, it was not until we had passed over the brow and through the western fringe of the tussac that we were able to see the west coast. Just where we emerged, the ground, at this point a bank of solid black peat, dropped away sharply to a plateau that lay twenty feet below and sloped gently down to the coast.

After a few seconds of stunned silence Pete exclaimed, "Good Lord!" Stretching away to the northern end of the island and down to the shore was a mass of black-browed albatross and rockhopper penguins, so densely packed that it was almost impossible to see the ground on which they were standing. Now Pete knew what had been causing that surf-like sound: this vast rookery of birds. The closer we came to it, the louder was the noise; and, as we stood, a few yards apart, among the birds, we could not hear each other speak. So closely packed were the birds that it would have been impossible to have walked very far through the colony without treading on birds, nests or eggs. By that time I had seen all the black-browed albatross rookeries in the Falklands, and there was no question that this was the largest. In addition, it was probably the Falklands' largest mixed colony of birds.

In 1965, on my second visit to Beauchêne, I had spent two days calculating the size of this rookery. Ground counts were used to calculate the density of the nesting birds, and aerial photographs taken from the helicopters of HMS *Protector* enabled the total area of the colony to be assessed. On my first visit to the island I had guessed that the rookery contained over a million birds; but, when calculations were complete, the figure that emerged was over three and a half million. This staggered me, but there seemed no reason to doubt the calculations. Dr Martin Holdgate suggested that I let him have a report on my findings for the journal *Polar Record*.

Zoologists and biologists generally seem reluctant to put a figure on the size of a large colony, and it was not long before I discovered why. In my report to Martin I made a grave mistake in not being specific about the method of calculation used and whether I was referring to breeding pairs, nests or individuals. In the article that appeared in *Polar Record*, the figures were mistakenly given as referring to pairs.

At about the same time I wrote a popular-type article about the bird life of the Falklands. It appeared in *Animals* magazine and was the first such article I had written. Again I made the mistake of not being specific enough, quoting my calculations and figures for the size of the Beauchêne rookery from my manuscript for the *Polar Record* article. As a result, the memory of one of the most magnificent sights I have ever seen recalls to me the pains and frustrations I subsequently had to endure in defending my calculations and descriptions of that colony.

The article in *Animals* brought a critical protest from Woods, whom I had known well when he worked in Stanley for a few years as a meteorological assistant. Woods was a keen bird man whom I admired for his critical attention to detail. In his letter to the editor of *Animals* he pulled the entire article to bits, giving special attention to the Beauchêne figures. More criticism was to follow: even Roddy Napier thought the figures grossly exaggerated, and Dr Lance Tickell, who had been working on black-browed albatross in South Georgia, was doubtful of my figures and wanted me to recheck carefully. What amazed me most about these criticisms was they were based not on any first-hand knowledge of Beauchêne Island and its rookeries, but on measurements and descriptions of the much smaller and less densely populated albatross colony on West Point Island. This was quite ridiculous, as no two rookeries are exactly alike. I took Woods's letter very much to heart, for at that time I saw it as endangering my hopes of continuing my work in the Falklands. My article had been written to give a broad picture of our wildlife; it was not meant as a detailed scientific analysis. Clearly, the one course I could take was to answer my critics with conclusive evidence, and by the time I had done this I had spent about £65 on defending an article for which I had been paid just over £50!

Beneath the tussac grass on Beauchêne was a deep layer of peat. The greatest depth that we found was over thirty feet, but I suspected that there were even deeper deposits. How long it had taken to form was impossible to tell, for, although it was easy to count the individual layers towards the top of the exposed bank (one year's fall of tussac leaves forming one layer), the lower layers were compressed into a solid mass that looked very much like coal. In most areas the rookery extended up to the base of the peat banks, where the birds nested on a layer of fine peat mould. This mould stretched several yards into the rookery, then gave way to rocky ground. I wondered how far out the tussac had once grown, for it appeared

Rockhopper Penguins

Adult Rockhopper penguin (*Eudyptes crestatus*).

that the rookery was slowly moving inland. Here and there the bank showed signs of having recently fallen away, and birds were establishing their nests on the top of the huge pieces of peat that had broken off. Most of the colonies I had seen appeared to be very gradually diminishing, but this one appeared to be growing.

Another unusual feature of the Beauchêne Island colony was that the terrain of which it made use was not of the type normally favoured by albatross. Usually these birds nest on high ground or on the sides of steep hills or cliffs, from which they can launch directly into flight on strong upward currents of air. Here, however, most albatross nested on gently sloping ground that gave them no assistance when taking off. On days when conditions were exceptionally calm, they seemed to be virtually grounded; but we later found that they had what can only be described as a runway.

This lay towards the centre of the island and was a long strip of open, beaten-down ground about 100 yards in length and running north-west to south-east. On one side the ground was thickly covered with rockhoppers and albatross, all jostling for space to nest. On the other side was a small colony of Gentoo penguins, and beyond them more albatross and penguins. I had often walked down this track and thought it marked a boundary between colonies, though there seemed no particular reason why this should be so. Later I discovered the truth. One very warm, calm day, as I was sitting close to the Gentoo colony filming a Johnny Rook stealing a young penguin chick, my attention was distracted by a number of albatross walking past me and laboriously making their way to one end of the strip. There groups of birds were assembled, and every few seconds, with huge wings flapping, a bird would run down the pathway, eventually lifting into the still air.

On my second visit to the island I had spent a night searching through tussac for species of petrel. On that occasion I had found considerable numbers of Wilson's petrel and a few diving petrels, but no others, which at the time surprised me. Now that I had plenty of time to look further, I made a point of sitting out on calm nights to see what birds came over when darkness fell. One evening from close to the hut, I saw the light shapes of prions circling the bay, but hunt as Pete and I did we could not find any signs of nesting birds.

My searches for prions had been concentrated on the area of tussac growing to the north of our camp site. This seemed the most likely area in which to find the nests of ground burrowing species. Conversely, the area of the Citadel, where the ground is covered with huge rock slabs, seemed far from suitable for such birds.

I had always been wary of the southern end of the island—in fact, Beauchêne as a whole is dangerous to walk over. Slabs of rock weighing many tons will at the touch of a foot suddenly pivot or sway. Cutting across the southern end of the island are deep fissures that one can easily span, but just as easily drop into. At one point there is a particularly wide fissure, which nearly cuts the island in two. At some time, this had been partly filled by a rock slide. Huge boulders weighing many tons are jammed in this gap, which, while not too difficult to cross during daylight, is far from easy to negotiate at night. South of this gap, which Pete and I named Boulder Corridor, is the Citadel, which from a distance seems almost totally devoid of birds. However, on close inspection we found large numbers of rockhopper penguins nesting in the shelter of the rock slabs. In the same area I came across the discarded eggshells of prions, and, on moving a few surface rocks, discovered that the rock underneath was loose, with many cavities, containing chicks, and stained by the passage of birds. In other places we found the same, indicating that probably the whole Citadel was used by prions. On inspecting the chicks, I took them to be thin-billed prions (*Pachyptila belcheri*), the only species of prion that was known to live in the Falklands.

Even though I knew that it would be difficult to visit the Citadel at night, I decided that this had to be done. We had powerful torches, but I thought that even with these it would be difficult to find the correct route across Boulder Corridor. To made things easier we decided to build cairns every few yards; and, on our way back from our first, daytime visit to the Citadel, we were kept busy marking a route.

Owing to execrable weather, it was several days before we were able to revisit the Citadel. In the meantime, we had torrential rain and—unusual in the Falklands—a thunderstorm; our time was fully occupied in mopping up. Our tents stood up to the weather well, but our efforts at making the hut watertight were not very success-ful, and eventually we had to take out a small section of the floor so that the mud and water could drain away. Needless to say, it was not feasible to travel about the island in such weather, and so for four days we were confined to base.

All of a sudden the weather changed and it became calm and hot. The whole island was now a mud bath, and as we walked through the rookeries our boots became caked with wet peat and guano. The dark peaty ground steamed with the heat, and the air became heavy with ammonia fumes. These were so strong that we had to keep away from the main rookery, and I wondered how the birds were able to stand them.

The tussac grass on Beauchêne was rich in colour, which suggested that it was thickly populated with birds and fed by their droppings. This was not so, and there seemed to be no other explanation that could account for the rich growth. Now the answer dawned on me: the ammonia fumes were rich in nitrogen, and, as they drifted over and condensed above the tussac, gave the grass a dressing of this nutrient. Perhaps the same happened when sea spray was carried by strong winds across the rookeries and onto the tussac.

We decided to return to the Citadel that same evening and wait for the return of the prions. We set off at 8.30 p.m., when there was still plenty of light, and, though the going was treacherous after such a lot of rain, we reached our destination about an hour later. As we were some 250 feet above sea level, with no shelter from the chill wind, we set to building a shelter wall from slabs of rock, then settled down to wait. Not until 11.45 p.m., when the last traces of light had left the sky, did we see the first prions sweeping back and forth over the area. Soon their weird calls were heard among the rocks beneath us, as pairs of birds reached their young. I had placed microphones in various cavities under the rocks, and, as I listened to their calls through the recorder, it was like being in some vast underground chamber. It was difficult to tell how many birds were flying above us, but there was a continual stream sweeping to and fro. In order to check the species, we started to prepare a mist net, but even as we stretched it out three birds were netted immediately. Close inspection was difficult by torchlight, so I decided to hold the birds until day. We stayed on the Citadel stack until 1.30 a.m., and still the prions were coming in from the sea, landing on the slabs, and disappearing below ground.

Heavy cloud now obscured the sky and produced an inky blackness all about us. We located our first stone cairn, but, search as we did, could not find any more. Knowing that, in order to keep clear of the numerous fissures, we had to keep to a narrow route down the centre of the stack, we were uneasy, and more than once the torch beam shone into an abyss, from the bottom of which came the distant sound of surf. At this we had no alternative but to turn back and try again. By the time we had safely crossed the corridor and were making our way over lower ground, it was nearly three o'clock. It had taken us twice as long to cover that route by night as it had by daylight. By the time we crawled into our sleeping bags, dawn was breaking, and the prions, having fed their young, were already well on their way out to sea.

I spent some time measuring the prions I had caught and then let two of them go, deciding to take only one specimen. This I skinned and carefully preserved, for I could not be sure that the birds were thin-billed prions. In daylight their feathers were much brighter than those of other prions I had handled, and their bills appeared much wider; but, as I had with me no details of the thin-billed prion, I could not be certain.

After I had returned to Stanley and compared specimens, I was in no doubt that the Beauchêne prions were different from the thin-billed variety, whose bill, shape, colour and size were not as those of the Beauchêne speciment. Eventually I concluded that the species most closely resembling this new find was the fairy prion (*Pachyptila turtur*), a species normally found in New Zealand waters. This discovery was exciting; but, though Dr Murphy and Dean Amadon accepted the evidence of my descriptions, tape recordings, and the one skin, many were sceptical, and it was not until after I had returned to Beauchêne four years later and gathered more information that the find was accepted. On this later visit to the island I was amazed to discover that the species was quite prolific all over the island; yet not one thin-billed prion could I find!

I was becoming increasingly concerned about the Falkland population of Johnny Rooks. Although there used to be considerable numbers of them on some of the Cape Horn islands, S. W. Johnson, author of *Birds in Chile* and an expert on the birds of that area, had no record that they had been sighted there recently. It thus appeared that the Falklands had become the last breeding ground for these hawks. Several times I considered proposing to the IUCN and WWF that the bird be viewed as an endangered species; but, though I was sure that numbers were low, I could not be sure exactly how low they were. Nonetheless, in classifying islands according to their worth as potential reserves, I gave priority to those supporting breeding populations of Johnny Rooks; and Beauchêne, which appeared to have more of these birds than any other island, headed my list. In some places their nests were only forty feet apart; and several birds were found nesting within a few feet of the rockhopper nests on which they preyed.

I was greatly concerned by the number of infertile Johnny Rook eggs that I came across. Often a complete clutch of eggs had been abandoned. I was never able to have these examined to discover the cause of their infertility, but suspected that DDT might be the explanation. In the Falklands hydrocarbons had for many years been used in sheep dips, and they continued to be used even when the use of such compounds was banned in England. The fact that traces of DDT had been discovered even in the tissue of Antarctic penguins suggested that penguins living in the Falklands were likely to be worse affected and that the Johnny Rooks feeding on them might well ingest sufficient hydrocarbons to cause infertility, thus further endangering the species' survival.

On my second visit to Beauchêne I had banded a number of Johnny Rooks, and I now hoped to find these. However, though on the advice of Lance Tickell I had used a colour system enabling individual birds to be identified, his and my work had been in vain, for not one ringed bird was found. Apart from the physical difficulties of ringing these birds, there is the additional problem of their curiosity at anything bright: a ringed bird will not be content to leave the ring in place, but will tug at it with its powerful beak. Once, when I ringed a number of Johnny Rooks on West Point Island, I was amazed to see these birds fly off to the nearest fence post and, within a minute or two, unwind the rings and fly away with them in their beaks! I hoped that this had been unusual, but clearly it had not been.

My discovery that there was no longer any large fur seal colony on Beauchêne Island, and apparently no fur seal there at all, made me particularly concerned to check the island carefully, to see if a few could be found. A number of helicopter flights round the island had revealed none; but on one of these flights we had discovered that what had appeared on aerial photographs as a bare patch in the tussac was in fact a deep hole, approximately 150 feet in diameter and about the same in depth. In the cliffs of the east coast, about 150 yards away, there opened a large cave, and it seemed that the cave and the hole might be connected. As no fur seal had been found elsewhere, I wondered if there might be a few in the cave, and whether this could be reached by way of the hole. I decided to find out.

The hole lay only about 300 yards from the camp site, but the journey there was one of the most gruelling treks through tussac I have ever made. So deep and thick was the grass that the only practicable ways of moving through it were by crawling on all fours beneath the tussac canopies, or by jumping from the top of one tussac stool to another. It took over an hour to cover the 300 yards.

One side of the hole was sheer, while the other dropped away at a steep angle. This side was thickly covered with tussac, and it seemed that it would be relatively easy to climb down. Halfway, however, we found that further progress was not feasible; so we sat down where we were, to watch and listen. Everything was still except for a low murmur of surf and the sound of sea water washing gently over the beach at the bottom (so proving that the cave was linked with the hole); but of seal there was no sign. Had there been any in the cave, we should have heard the call of a pup, the bark or cough of an adult, or the sound of the animals swimming. Later we climbed to a point from where we could look into the cave entrance, but not one seal did we see.

Even though the fur seal colonies had gone, I was still anxious to determine where they had been. Unfortunately, the inscriptions at Blinns Bay and some sealing relics that we found in the same area told us only where the sealers probably had lived, not where the seal had been found. The only real clue I had to the location of the colonies was given by *Fanning's Voyages Round the World* (1834), which described a rock at the north-east end of Beauchêne as "covered with fur seal", and contained a print showing seal being hunted on the island. On our helicopter flights I had paid special attention to the area described, but was unable to pinpoint the place illustrated. However, when later I visited the area on foot, I found a place that resembled the illustration and had the appearance of a typical fur seal haunt, with rocky ledges worn smooth by the passage of animals over a great number of years. Now everything was still, with not a sign of seal.

It is often said that illicit sealing must have been the cause of the fur seal's disappearance from Beauchêne, but my own view is that the two sealers from Stanley who visited the island in 1919 took the last remaining animals. These sealers were on the island for nearly two months, but returned with only eleven skins—a good indication that there were then very few seal left.

Sealion, though, have managed to survive on the island. However, though we found plenty of evidence that large herds had once
lived there, a search of the entire coastline revealed only about 150
animals. This provided further sad evidence of the decline of the
species in the Falklands.

When we had been on Beauchêne Island for just over a fortnight, we
received word from Stanley that HMS *Protector* wished to speak to
us. We were surprised, as we thought the ship was somewhere in the
Antarctic; but we were even more surprised when we made contact
and were informed that the ship would pick us up later the same
day. This was about a week earlier than planned, and we could only
assume there was some emergency.

At 8.20 p.m. we were lifted off the island. The evening was grey
and overcast and drizzle had plagued our packing, but I was nonetheless sorry to be leaving. As we boarded *Protector* the ship's siren
gave us a welcome blast, and shortly afterwards Captain Sandford
told us that he and his crew were relieved to see us safely back on
board. Having not heard anything of us on the ship's radio, many
had wondered whether we had in fact survived!

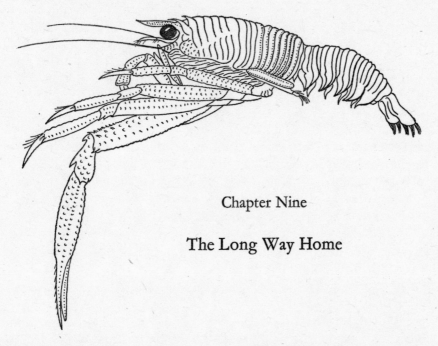

Chapter Nine

The Long Way Home

Since my arrival in the Falklands I had been hoping that at some time I should have the chance to take a good look at the South American continent. On my trip to England in 1963 I had seen a little of Argentina but not much else, having travelled by aeroplane. Now that I was again to return to England, with no certainty of being able to come back to the Falklands soon, I decided to take my chance while it offered and travel overland by Land Rover to North America, seeing on the way some of the wild places I had heard about and how they were being conserved. However, it seemed unwise to make the trip alone, and I was not sure whom I could get to join me. Eventually Pete, my companion on Beauchêne Island, his wife Marie, and Ann Gisby, a teacher friend—all of whom were due to go home to England after completing their teaching contracts—said that they would come.

One of the biggest problems was currency for the trip. At that time the Government limited to £50 per person the amount that could be taken out for exchange. In January 1967 I received the documents I required in order to take the vehicle through South America and, armed with these as proof of our intentions, approached Thompson, the Colonial Secretary, to see if the allowance might be raised. Finally it was agreed to accept the expedition as a semi-scientific one, with an allowance of £100 per person—£400 overall.

I spent much of January working on the Land Rover, desperately trying to put it back together, for I had stripped the vehicle down and virtually rebuilt the engine. At the same time I had other preparations to make and had still to find time to sail *Gleam* to West Point Island, where Roddy Napier was to look after her.

The original plan had been for the four of us plus the Land Rover to leave Stanley on 20 February, sailing to Montevideo in Uruguay. However, as the time approached it became obvious that I would not be ready, so Annie, Marie and Pete sailed alone to Montevideo to await my arrival with the Land Rover in mid March.

Before sailing *Gleam* to West Point, a journey of about 150 miles, I had to see that she was in good order. She was an excellent sea boat and I had every confidence in her ability to make the journey, but Eddie Anderson, an expert on local sailing who was to go with me, was concerned about the strength of the existing wheelhouse. I therefore decided to replace the wheelhouse with a new one, and this took four days to do.

On the day when the work was finished, the weather was fine so we decided to start the trip that same evening and, making use of a good moon, sail on through the night. As the wind was from the south-west, we set our course along the north coast of East Falkland, leaving Stanley at 8.35 p.m. on 22 February. Two hours later we were clearing Volunteer Rocks, just in time to see hundreds of fur seal leaving for their fishing grounds.

Later the wind dropped completely and the sea lay calm and bathed in moonlight. Our wake was continually alive with flashes of light from the vast numbers of minute phosphorescent marine creatures that we churned up to the surface. So bright were these flashes that it seemed almost as though we were passing through an electrical storm and seeing it reflected in the water.

At 7.00 a.m. we rounded Cape Dolphin, from where we could see thousands of prions feeding in the tidal stream that swept up the Falkland Sound. Fortunately conditions were still calm as we changed course for the south-west, moving out and into the Sound. Close by I saw the pillar-shaped Eddystone Rock, where fur seal had once bred, and I wished that there were time to visit it.

We now aimed for the narrow Tamar Pass between Pebble Island and West Falkland. The Tamar forms a bottleneck, and as the tide flows to the north the mass of water between the two islands is squeezed out through the pass, the reverse occurring as the tide turns. Halfway across the Falkland Sound, Eddie realised that we would miss slack water and arrive at the Tamar as the tide was flowing against us.

At 10 a.m. we were approaching the entrance to the pass, and what a sight it was! Foaming through it was a stream of water running twelve to eighteen inches on top of the sea's surface. How fast the tide was running we had no idea, but, as it was nearly full moon, the tides would be near their strongest. Large boats with a great deal more power sometimes had trouble in going through the pass against the tide, so our chances were slim. Nonetheless, Eddie thought it worth a try, so we edged our way towards the stream.

No sooner had *Gleam*'s bow cut into the edge of the race than she was gripped by the flow, heeled over, and was swept round 180 degrees. As she turned the stream caught her stern and she did a complete circle. For several minutes there was no response on the wheel and the propeller churned the water furiously as we were swept back out into the Sound; then gradually the motor took over and we slid out of the race. To change our course for the north of Pebble Island was out of the question, as we calculated that it would put us in a more difficult area by nightfall; so we settled to wait till the tide slackened.

We anchored on the south side of Tamar Pass in the shelter of West Falkland. Pebble Island, on the other side of the pass, lay only about 100 yards away. Through the Tamar and on the other side of the promontory by which we were anchored was a sheltered harbour called Robinson's Bay, which William Horton Smyley, an American with a reputation for being a rogue and pirate, had used as a base for his activities in the early nineteenth century. Smyley established himself in the Falklands during the 1830s and, with a group of runaway seamen, operated a business in cattle hunting and illicit sealing.

While we waited for the tide to slacken I pondered over Smyley's reason for picking Robinson's Bay as a base. The more I thought, the more I realised how clever he had been. Besides being a well-sheltered harbour with a clear view of the only two approaches, the bay had another advantage. Any vessel approaching the passage against the tide would have no hope of getting through; and thus a vessel anchored in the bay would have time on its side in preparing its escape.

Later the tide slackened sufficiently to allow us to make another attempt. This time we slowly made headway against the flow, and, at two or three knots with the engine at full power, *Gleam* cleared the pass. At about 7.30 p.m. we were making our way into Byron Sound with a strong wind against us and a mounting sea threatening to make the rest of the journey uncomfortable. Having lost a lot of time at the Tamar, we could no longer reach West Point that day, and therefore decided to head for Carcass Island. By the time we were well up Byron Sound it was dark, with the moon hidden by thick cloud; we now had to rely on the compass and Eddie's knowledge of the area. At 11 p.m. we eventually anchored at Carcass, having been sailing for about twenty hours. This, apparently, was a record run for a sailing boat, but one that could have been bettered had we not been held up at the Tamar Pass.

The next few days were spent at Carcass, and as the tides were exceptionally good I brought *Gleam* up against the jetty in order to dry her out and give her a coat of anti-fouling. I was staggered to see how much weed had grown on her since she was last beached, and I realised how much better her run could have been without that.

Eddie having had to fly back to Stanley the day after our arrival at Carcass, I set off for West Point on my own, against an unfavourable wind and tide. I was using the engine, with the foresail to help keep the boat steady, when, half way across Byron Sound, a sail halyard broke. During my attempts to mend this I realised how stupid I was to try to sail the boat on my own in such conditions. *Gleam* had over 500 square feet of sail and it was only when conditions were fair that it was feasible to manage her single-handed. While fixing the halyard I let her run with the wind and tide, and in an amazingly short time I was way off course. Had the engine failed, I should have had trouble indeed in getting the boat under sail. It was a small incident, but another lesson learned.

Now that I had *Gleam* at West Point, I was anxious to use the opportunity to look at some of the smaller islands in the area. A day or two after my arrival at West Point, Roddy, Ted Robson and Riley Short set off with me on *Gleam* to Split Island, which lies south of West Point. This island I knew had foxes on it, but of greater interest to me was the fact that Split had never been stocked with grazing animals.

The island, which takes its name from a deep cut in its centre, is wedge-shaped, with tremendous cliffs on one side, sloping down to shelving slabs at sea level on the other. This slope faces due north, thus obtaining the full benefit of the sun, and is richly covered with vegetation. Blue grass (*Poa alopecurus*) predominates, with other native grasses dispersed through it; but what struck me most were the remains of flowers, mainly primula and orchids. Here was an island that clearly illustrated what many others must have looked like before these delicate and more palatable plants were eaten out by sheep and cattle.

It is ironic that only two days after I stood on Split looking at its undamaged flora, I was myself to assist in stocking an unspoilt island with sheep. The island in question was Elephant Jason, which along with South Jason had been leased out for sheep grazing immediately after having been declared a sanctuary. I had strongly condemned this as short-sighted and wrong (see Chapter 7), but had hardly imagined that I would lend a hand to what I had condemned.

Riley Short, who lived on West Point, had obtained the lease, and at the time of my arrival on the island was making arrangements to transport sheep to the Elephant Jason. The vessel *Malvinas* had been hired for the purpose, and early on 3 March succeeded in reaching the island, where we put ashore some 150 sheep. Though I could hardly feel easy about assisting, I was glad to have the chance to spend a few hours on the island.

What I saw made me even more certain how short-sighted it was to allow the island to be stocked. A perfect belt of tussac grass surrounded a plain covered mainly with two types of blue grass and a large amount of fern. Yet nearly twenty years earlier, in November 1949, Elephant Jason had been struck by lightning, and some parts had burned for two years; even now the ground was still soft underfoot where vegetation had yet to stabilise the ash. This was one argument I had put forward for leaving the island alone; in this state it was still subject to erosion, and, if sheep were allowed to overgraze, the results would be disastrous. As it was not intended to erect fencing and the sheep were to be visited only once a year, for shearing, the chances that the island would survive erosion were poor. Further, Elephant Jason, like other islands in the group, was exceptionally dry, and, though I walked right round the island, I found no spring or pond, or even a mud patch. To my amazement, the lack of water supplies for the sheep was treated as a minor consideration.

On West Point the following day, I stood on Cape Terrible looking out towards the Jason group. Close to where I stood were the remains of a try works, where sealers and penguin oilers had rendered down thousands of penguins and collected hundreds of sealskins. Those days were gone and the industries would never return. Most of the islanders I knew condemned those industries, and yet the destruction of the islands' resources continued, though in a different and subtler way. Those sheep I had helped put on Elephant Jason would in time destroy much of the natural vegetation and the habitat of many birds. It was an indirect form of depredation; it would be gradual; but the final results would be the same.

In a few days I would be leaving the Falklands, but I knew that I had to come back. There had to be a way to illustrate the folly of what was happening, to show that the benefits that accrued from such ill-conceived schemes as stocking Elephant Jason with sheep were far too small and limited to justify the destruction that they involved. A lot was being lost, and perhaps irretrievably.

On 13 March 1967 I left Port Stanley, and late at night on the 16th reached Montevideo, where I was to rejoin Annie, Marie and Pete. The Land Rover and equipment were landed the following day. No sooner had the vehicle been landed than it was impounded, and it was only with the help of a friend who lived in Uruguay—plus many packets of English cigarettes—that we were able to obtain its release. On 19 March our journey commenced and we crossed the Rio de la Plata into Argentina.

Owing to strained relations between the Falkland Islands and Argentina (which claimed the islands), we took care not to give any indication that we came from the Falklands, or Islas Malvinas as the Argentinians called them. The Land Rover was given a new British registration plate, and we approached the Argentinian customs with trepidation.

To our surprise and relief we experienced few problems. A few years earlier an Argentinian airliner had been hijacked by a group of nationalists and flown to the Falklands, where, there being no airstrip, it had had to make a forced landing. We got to know the pilot, Ernesto Garcia, quite well, and, on explaining to the customs authorities that he was the person we would be visiting, all formalities were dropped and we were ushered through. It thus turned out that coming from the Falklands was more of a help than a hindrance, and we in fact found that people were much more interested in learning something of the islands than in arguing about the sovereignty issue.

In order to travel up through South America we had to follow the Pan American Highway, which lies on the west side of the continent. This meant travelling across Argentina, then over the Andes into Chile or Bolivia, before we could actually head north. We decided to cross to Chile by way of Mendoza at the foot of the Andes.

With the help of Francisco Erize, a naturalist friend of mine living in Buenos Aires, we planned our route across Argentina so as to see as much wildlife as possible. I was staggered by the number of species we saw, especially types of hawk and wildfowl. Vagrants from the South American continent are fairly common in the Falklands, and now I realised why. However, I learned from Francisco that there is generally very little interest in conservation in Argentina. Few reserves have been established and attempts at stimulating interest have so far met with little response. Sad to say, I found this to be the case throughout South America.

On 8 April we crossed the Andes into Chile, where I met the well-known ornithologist S. W. Johnson; and shortly afterwards we were on our way north along the Pacific coast, through the Atacama desert into Peru. For many years there was a very successful guano industry along this coast, but, when it was discovered that fertiliser could be produced direct from the fish (mainly anchovy) that went to form the guano, the birds whose guano had been collected were cut out of the cycle and are now decreasing as the fishermen take their food. Travelling along the Peruvian coast, we came across several places where just a few years previously guano had been harvested; now the sites had been abandoned by both industry and birds. Instead we came across vast stockpiles of bagged fishmeal, representing thousands of tons of the anchovy on which the cormorants and other birds had depended.

In Peru I wanted very much to see some vicuña, and, as we found none in the Andes near Lake Titicaca, we returned to the coast and carried on to Lima, from where I hoped to go by another route into the Andes and over to the jungle areas on the east. However, on being advised that the route would be waterlogged at that time of year, we instead decided to fly to Pucallpa, one of Peru's jungle towns. Up to the time of making this trip we had still not been able to contact any local experts on wildlife, which was a great disappointment. Our only contact in Pucallpa was a missionary connected with the School of Linguistics at a place called Yarina Cocha. We had been led to understand that we could probably make a base at the school and from there travel some way out into the jungle. This we were able to do to a certain extent, but were sadly disappointed in what we found at the school.

The name of Maria Koepcke had been mentioned to us before our journey up to Pucallpa. Both she and her husband were zoologists who worked for the Museo Javier Prado in Lima. Unfortunately we did not succeed in contacting them until after our return from the jungle. On hearing of our visit to Pucallpa, Maria Koepcke reacted much as our experience of the place might have led us to expect. However, though we had seen few birds there, I had come back with a sizable collection of recordings—and mosquito bites, which were an experience of their own!

Maria Koepcke mentioned Ian Grimwood, who, as a conservationist, had been sent out to Peru as a technical adviser on behalf of the British Ministry of Overseas Development. His name was familiar to me but I had never met him, and it was a miracle that I managed to meet him in Lima. Annie and I set off armed with directions on where we might find him, but we became hopelessly lost and eventually began to think of giving up. Stopping to ask directions, we found that, of all the people in Lima we could have asked, we had actually chosen Ian Grimwood himself! It was an amazing meeting —all the more so as we found that he and his wife were just about to return to England; and it resulted in a long friendship. Ian had spent some three years in Peru advising the Peruvian Servicio Forestal y de Caza on the establishment of a wildlife reserve in the jungle.

I was staggered when Ian told us that it had taken him all that time to find a comparatively untouched piece of jungle, and that, by the time that it was protected as a reserve, even that would have been so violated by skin hunters that much of its value would have been lost. On leaving Pucallpa, I had noticed that many of the men boarding the aircraft carried nothing but roughly tied bundles of animal skins. These men were apparently the links between dealer and Indian. They travelled into the jungle to buy skins from Indians and then resold them to dealers in places like Lima. I had seen only a minute portion of the trade, but, if this was carried out from every town in the Peruvian jungle, it is no wonder that Ian was so concerned.

On 29 May we reached the border of Ecuador, having seen no vicuña during our stay in Peru. The border between Ecuador and Peru is one of the most natural I have ever seen, being marked by

Red-backed Buzzard

Female Red-backed buzzard (*Buteo Polyosoma*). This study was taken from one of a pair holding a territory close to Stanley. Although breeding sites of these beautiful hawks can be found on many hill-top ridges and prominent rocky outcrops, the species is not common. Unlike some other birds of prey, this hawk is perhaps better understood by farmers as one that feeds mainly on rodents, hares, rabbits, small birds but does not prey on live sheep or lambs.

the most dramatic changes in terrain and climate. Within a mile or two, dry desert (on the Peruvian side) changes to semi-jungle country (on the Ecuadorian side). The principal reason for this is that the cold Humboldt current swings away from the coast just by the border.

The change in climate and terrain affected our camping arrangements, which along the dry desert coast had been no problem: we had simply driven off the road. Now the land along the roadside was thick with vegetation and we often had to spend hours searching for a suitable place to stop, sometimes seeking help from local landowners.

By the time we reached Quito, Pete and Marie were both suffering badly from stomach upsets, and the strain of spending long hours cramped together in the short-wheelbase Rover was beginning to tell. It was therefore decided that Pete and Marie (who in addition had received news that her father was seriously ill), would have to break the trip and fly back to England. The situation was critical, for it left Annie and me on our own, with a long way to go and the problem of very little money.

As it was not possible to reach Central America by road (the Darien region of Panama being the problem) it had been planned that we would drive to Barranquilla in Colombia and take ship from there to Panama. However, at that time Barranquilla was supposed to be having a lot of trouble from bandits, and I was under pressure to miss out Colombia altogether. When Marie and Pete found that they could no longer continue the trip, I agreed to ship from the Ecuadorian port of Guayaquil instead.

In Quito I briefly met the British Ambassador, Mr Corley-Smith, who was an authority on the birds of Ecuador. He told me of a scheme that the WWF had put forward for establishing a wildlife reserve on the equator, and, though I believe that he felt that other parts of the country were more valuable and deserving of protection, he suggested that we visit the proposed reserve and see what we thought of it. From what little we did see of it, I was forced to conclude that no great advantage would be gained from the scheme, for the region was farmed and quite heavily populated.

On 6 June, Annie and I bid farewell to Marie and Pete, and left for Guayaquil, where we embarked on a vessel bound for Panama. Even though we still had a long way to go and not a great deal of time or money at our disposal, I was determined to keep as closely as possible to our original plan, which was to see as much as we could. Throughout the rest of the journey, we continued to turn aside and try to learn something of the areas through which we were travelling. Often we would stay in one place for several days, recording and photographing.

However, soon after our arrival in Panama, where we spent some time on Barro Colorado Island, a jungle research station operated by the Smithsonian Institute, the rainy season set in. I had planned the journey so that our time in South America should coincide with the best seasons; now the expected change came and every day we experienced a downpour. Our equipment and clothing were continually damp, and camping became a trial. Many times we were forced to pitch the tent while it was raining, and for desperate want of sleep crawl in regardless of how wet things were.

It took us three weeks to travel through Panama, Costa Rica, Nicaragua, El Salvador and Guatemala. In Guatemala, in an effort to escape from the heat and rains, we decided to take the high mountain route—one we had been warned to avoid because of bandits. Considering the state that we and the vehicle were in, we thought that no bandit would take a second look at us, and certainly we experienced no such trouble at all. In addition, the route, though very rough in parts, proved beautiful, and the weather was cool and rainless.

On 4 July we crossed into Mexico, and I remember thinking that now, at last, we were on the last lap. That, however, was before I had worked out just how far it was to the United States border! Driving through Mexico was exhausting, and, with stops, took us over a fortnight. Reaching Mexicali, at the border with the United States, we gave a sigh of relief. Now, we thought, we should no longer have any problems finding diesel fuel and areas to camp, and everything else would be easier. Our delight at crossing into the States was written all over our faces, but it made little impression on the American immigration officer, who, taking one look at my passport, said, "You can't enter; your visa expired a few days ago".

Already the Rover had been entered into the USA, the Mexican authorities having stamped the vehicle carnet as cleared from Mexico. They had also cancelled my immigration card and stamped my passport. Both Annie and I were very hungry, and the temperature was 120°F, but this did not assist our pleading with American officialdom. We finished up in no man's land between the two frontiers, unable to take the Rover back into Mexico, or to enter the United States. It was hurriedly decided that Annie would stay with the vehicle while I went back into Mexico to find an American Consul who could renew the visa.

At first the Mexicans were reluctant to let me re-enter, as my immigration card had been cancelled. However, perhaps to show they were not so officious as the Americans, they eventually agreed to let me pass. Many hours later, feeling much the worse for wear but in possession of a new visa, I returned to the American border. By a strange twist of fate, it had all turned out for the best, for, on hearing of the trip, the Consul had offered to issue a visa permitting me to do certain types of work in the United States. As we now had virtually no money left, this was indeed a blessing.

After a few days travelling in the United States, we realised how wrong we had been in expecting to have no more problems in finding fuel and camping areas. In fact, the difficulties increased. To find diesel fuel, which in America is hardly ever stocked at normal filling stations, we had to follow the main truck routes, filling our tank at trucking stations. This often caused amusement, for we would drive up alongside some huge truck that might be taking several hundred gallons, while all we wanted was eight or nine! Many times our search for diesel involved driving many miles off route, and more than once we had to obtain supplies at bulk depots. In addition, we were so short of money that we could allow ourselves only three dollars a day for fuel and food. Consequently, we kept ourselves going on eggs, milk, margarine and bread, and occasionally chicken backs!

The problem of camping was one of cost more than anything else. There were plenty of well-equipped sites, but the fee for using these was more than our daily budget for fuel and food. Camping outside these sites was generally not permitted, so again we had the problem of finding somewhere each night. When things became too difficult we would wait until dark and then take to some highway verge, moving early in the morning, before we could be discovered.

For a few days we stopped at Santa Cruz on the Californian coast, where I arranged to meet Dr Richard Peterson, a biologist at Santa Cruz University. Though this was our first meeting, we had already been in correspondence, owing to our mutual interest in fur seal.

It so happened that, at the time of our arrival in Santa Cruz, Dick Peterson was just about to leave for Ano Nuevo Island, where the university was carrying out biological research on Californian sealion, Steller's sealion and Northern elephant seal. Having never before seen these animals in the wild, Annie and I were delighted when asked if we would like to make the trip, which was made even more enjoyable by the fact that we did not go merely as spectators. When we arrived at Ano Nuevo the researchers were preparing for the task of catching and tagging Steller's sealion pups, a job that was new to them and at which I could be of assistance. As I helped carry out this work, I imagined that I was on Volunteer Rocks, being reminded of them by the cool wind blowing off the sea, the smell of kelp, and the clamour of seal.

From Santa Cruz we went on to San Francisco, where we spent several nights sleeping in an office-*cum*-studio at Pier 1½ in the waterfront. We were feeling rather down and out, but our stay in San Francisco was nonetheless to prove of great value.

In travelling about California we met a remarkable number of people interested in wildlife, and were always being introduced to more. One introduction led us to the Californian Academy of Sciences in Golden Gate Park, San Francisco, where we met Dr Lindsay and Dr Orre, both of whom had a very keen interest in the wildlife, and especially the marine mammals, of the Falklands. Finding so much interest made me realise that, even if support for conservation measures was lacking in the islands, it certainly existed elsewhere. These meetings at the Academy were only short, but they proved the basis of some very worthwhile contacts.

Before leaving the Falklands I had selected about fifteen photographs illustrating the character and wildlife of the islands. I had done this very much as an afterthought, and the pictures were mainly proof prints of no special quality. However, these were to save us financially and take us right across North America.

In San Francisco we earned a few dollars by writing a newspaper article on the Falklands, illustrating this with the photographs I had brought with me. This was the first of perhaps fifteen such articles, nearly every one about the Falklands. Contrary to what we had expected, few editors seemed interested in the journey: in fact, we began to wonder if they believed we had driven so far! For every newspaper we produced a different article, yet the same photos were copied time and again. I began to feel like a travelling salesman, for at every town we came to, I immediately bought a newspaper, looked for the address of the editorial office, and then commenced business. Normally I would have found this sort of thing difficult, but, knowing the importance of earning a few dollars, I became as determined to sell a story as a reporter is to obtain one. The most we ever earned for a single article was about twenty dollars, and in some cases the editor paid us from his own pocket. The total amount was little, but sufficient for us to be able to keep our heads above water.

Mid August saw us travelling between Vancouver and Toronto, having already driven some 20,000 miles. Up till then the only trouble we had had with the Land Rover—barring the many punctures we had had in South and Central America—was in California, where we had to stop for a day in order to replace a piece on the starter motor. Now, in Toronto, we experienced more trouble, and this kept me puzzled for several days. However, eventually I found that the problem was no more than a cracked pin in the mechanical linkage of the clutch—a pin that took literally two or three minutes to replace and cost only a few cents!

While we were delayed in Toronto, we found our way into the offices of the Canadian Broadcasting Corporation's Natural History Unit. Again new contacts were made, and we became firm friends with John Livingstone, Bill Banting and Bill Gunn, all of whom were keenly interested in the Falklands and very conservation-minded. We learned a lot from them, especially about the production of wildlife films, and they persuaded me that I ought to attempt a film on wildlife in the Falklands. At the same time we progressed from newspaper articles to radio and TV broadcasts. This gave us a final boost financially, taking us through to New York without having to write more articles.

On Saturday 2 September our journey came to an end at Dean Amadon's house in New Jersey. The drive had taken nearly six months and we had travelled 22,000 miles. We were both very tired, especially Ann, who had been suffering from earache, and after a day or two it was arranged for her to fly to England while I stayed in New Jersey to follow up more contacts, particularly in New York, and earn a little more money to pay for shipping the Land Rover to London.

While I was staying with Dean Amadon, an unexpected telephone call sparked off a chain of events that was to prove decisive for my return to the Falklands. Involved in this was the Lindblad Travel organisation, of which I had first learned earlier that year, and which had operated an Antarctic expedition for tourists, using a Chilean vessel. Most of these tourists were keen amateur naturalists and it had occurred to me that the organisation might be interested in arranging a similar trip to the Falklands. This would show the

Falklanders the extent of interest in the islands' wildlife and might also be of some economic benefit. Unfortunately, I had received no reply to my letter to Lindblad Travel, but now that I was on the organisation's doorstep I was determined to try again.

The crucial phone call was from Roger Tory Peterson, a person whom I had never met or corresponded with, but whom I knew to be one of America's leading ornithologists. He had learned of my arrival in the area and of my interest in wildlife, and wanted to talk to me about the Falklands. What is more, he had acted as a leader on one of the Lindblad expeditions. When I explained to him my idea for an expedition to the Falklands, he was delighted; and just a few days later I was discussing with Lindblad Travel a plan for combining a visit to the islands with an expedition to Antarctica and southern Chile the following February.

I had long before decided that I would go back to the Falklands, but exactly how and when I had not known until that meeting in New York. Now one of my main hopes, that more people than just a few scientists would visit the islands to view wildlife, was being realised, and I knew that I had to get back to the Falklands before February. The work as such would not bring me any more than a month's salary, but it was something positive.

A lot of my time in New York was spent visiting various publishing houses in an attempt to create interest in the Falklands and obtain commissions for articles or photographs. Dean Amadon suggested that I approach the editor of the museum journal *Natural History*, and this resulted in an invitation to write an article on conservation in the islands. In similar fashion, I saw Les Line, editor of *Audubon Magazine*, and, while at the Audubon Society offices, I met the Society's president, Mr Clements. We discussed the Falklands and its conservation problems and he suggested that I see the Executive Director of the WWF American Appeal, Mr Herbert Mills. He thought Mr Mills would be interested to hear of my plans to return to conservation work in the islands and might be able to obtain for me a further WWF grant to assist the project.

It was arranged that I should meet Herbert Mills in his New York hotel at 8 a.m. on 13 September; on the same day I had also to meet Mr Andrew Brown of the National Geographic Society in Washington. To keep my appointment with Mills, I left Dean's house in New Jersey at around 6.00 a.m. I had been warned that Mills was a fairly high-powered type, but was surprised when our discussion was held simultaneously with an intermittent telephone conversation with someone in Switzerland! Nonetheless it was an enjoyable meeting and Mills was obviously very interested in my plans.

After this I left by train for Washington for my meeting with Andrew Brown. The purpose of the meeting was to discuss the possibility of an article, but on learning of my plans Brown thought that I should also see Dr Carmichael, head of the Society's research programmes, to see whether I could obtain a grant. I now look back with some amusement to that meeting with Dr Carmichael, though it showed me that I would not be getting any assistance from academic institutions. Opening the interview, Dr Carmichael asked me the meaning of two very long scientific terms that I had never heard before. I replied that I hadn't the faintest idea what they meant. I was then asked what academic qualifications I had in zoology or biology; again I gave him a negative answer. Clearly, I was expected to have such qualifications before I could even be considered by the Society's projects board. To me the situation was rather ridiculous: interest had been shown in my work, but I could not obtain support without paper qualifications. I pointed out to Carmichael that the projects I was carrying out did not require such things. The conservation work that had to be done was basic ground work involving a great number of simple field jobs, which a person with academic qualifications would probably not wish to do anyway.

During my last few days in the United States I wrote a travel article on the Falklands for the *New York Times*—an article that was later to have some amusing repercussions. Then, after seeing the Land Rover delivered to the New York docks for shipment to England, I flew back to London.

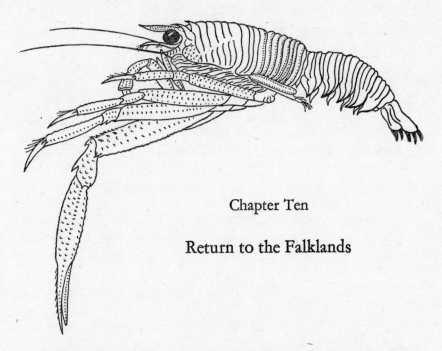

Chapter Ten

Return to the Falklands

I was looking forward to getting back to England and seeing the family—particularly the children, whom I had missed very much. They and Irene were at the farm in Essex, but during the time I spent there it became clear that Irene and I could no longer live together and that a parting was inevitable. I knew Annie wanted to go back to the Falklands and was prepared to do so for my sake, but she did not say so until I had discovered how things were with Irene. When finally she learned that the relationship between Irene and me would not mend, she decided to return to the islands on a further teaching contract.

Looking back, I believe I got through those months in England only by being so involved in all the work I had accumulated. A lot of letters had to be written to the Falklands to organise the Lindblad trip; I had a number of paintings to do for one of Lindblad Travel's expedition ships; and there were also articles to write. I spent a great deal of time in London trying to interest publishers in my ideas for a book about the wildlife of the Falklands. However, the situation was always the same: initially there was a great enthusiasm, but, as soon as the population of the islands was known to be only 2,000, the interest vanished.

I discussed with Sir Hugh Elliott, then Secretary of the Ecology Commission, my hopes for returning to the islands, but nothing materialised. It seemed, as Dr Martin Holdgate had already told me, that my lack of academic qualifications was likely to prevent my obtaining any financial support. I knew that Martin had seen Mr Thompson, the Falklands Colonial Secretary, in London some months before and that my projects had been discussed. I had not always been very diplomatic in my approaches to the Colonial Secretary, and on some issues, notably the seal survey, had been an embarrassment to the Government. I wondered how Thompson had reacted.

One of my main interests in returning to the islands was to continue the work on seal, but I knew this was something that I could not do without proper support. Richard Peterson and I had discussed this at length, and eventually it was suggested that he, as a biologist, should obtain the financial backing, and that I, under his direction, should carry out the fieldwork. In June, Richard had written to the Colonial Secretary mentioning his wish to carry out studies on fur seal and indicating that he would be utilising my knowledge. In reply, he was told that he would be welcome to visit the islands to carry out a study, but that, as I had now left the Falklands, he should get in touch with Dr E. A. Smith of the British Antarctic Survey, who was in possession of a good deal of information on Southern pinnipeds. I knew very well that, except for a brief visit to Stanley, Smith had not worked on Falkland seal and that the information was probably my own survey report held by the Government. Later I received a letter from another biologist, Emmerson, whom I had once met. He explained that he had plans well in hand for a study of the Falklands' fur seal and sealion and that his plans had been approved by both Dr Smith and the Governor of the Falklands.

I began seriously to wonder if in my keenness to return and work on seal I had again upset the proverbial apple cart. The answer came in a letter from Smith, who said that the programme proposed by Emmerson made sense to the Governor and was therefore likely to receive "official financial support". On the question of my own work on wildlife, he wrote, "if it is a preservation approach I am not surprised at the difficulties in enlisting support". Finally, "At present I am not persuaded that it is best for you to enlist American financial support for work on the fur seal in the Falkland Islands. As you realise, we have personnel and have carried the matter a good way with the Falkland Islands Government". I cannot remember exactly how I felt at the time, but I was very disappointed and could not help but wonder whether I was not, in fact, wanted to return to the islands. What eventually became of the Smith and Emmerson scheme I do not know, for it was never carried out. My own hopes for working on fur seal suffered a final blow when I received the sudden and very upsetting news that Richard Peterson had died. His death was a great loss to the world of seal biology.

Before I had left for New York, Herbert Mills had asked me to submit a project description and request for funds from the WWF. In this I stated my plans for surveying the smaller islands in the archipelago to establish their value as nature reserves, and my ideas for showing what the Falklands could offer both scientists and tourists. While still in England I received news that the Executive Committee of the WWF American Appeal had tentatively approved a grant of $6,000. I was staggered by the news and, although the grant had yet to be finally approved, my hopes were high.

On 4 January 1968 I left London for Buenos Aires, from where I continued to Puerto Montt in Chile. There I met up with the Lindblad expedition group led by Roger Tory Peterson. On the following day we set sail on the *Navarino*, a rather old Chilean vessel, and a few days later reached Puerto Natales, further down the coast. This area struck me as one of the most beautiful areas I had yet seen in South America, and its nickname "Switzerland of South America" was well deserved. At Natales we left the ship and went into the Paine Mountain area, which lies at the southern end of the Andes. There much of the vegetation and many of the bird species are the same as in the Falklands, even though the terrain is different from there. By 16 January we had sailed through the Beagle Channel and out to Hermite, Nuevo, and Wollaston islands. This was one region I had often wanted to look at, for Johnny Rooks were once common on these islands, though there no more. Later we were off Cape Horn and the Diego Ramirez rocks, heading for the Drake Passage and the Antarctic in the type of weather for which the Horn is infamous.

So violent did conditions become that early on the morning of the 18th a hydraulic piston on the steering gear of the *Navarino* broke. For several hours the ship drifted helplessly in what was now a very heavy sea. At first, efforts to bring the manual steering into operation had no success, and only when the Captain was preparing to send out a distress call was the ship brought under control with temporary steerage. So severe was the damage that *Navarino* had to make her way to Punta Arenas for repairs. This led to the cancellation of the rest of the expedition.

A second expedition, led by Peter Scott, was due to join the *Navarino* on 1 February. A few days before this I heard that repairs to the steering gear were complete and that the trip could therefore be made. I had last met Peter Scott at Peakirk, shortly after the Severn Wildfowl Trust had purchased the grounds from my father. Meeting again in a place like Punta Arenas seemed quite incredible, especially as we would be journeying together to the Falklands.

This expedition party was composed largely of English people, and their enthusiasm for wildlife made the time I spent with them most memorable. At the same time, I had ample opportunity for informal discussions with Peter Scott on conservation in the Falklands. This was his first visit to the islands, and, though he and his wife Philippa wanted it to be informal, I knew that he was almost bound to be approached officially, for his views on conservation. Because of this, I wanted to make sure that he had a clear picture of the situation in the islands.

On 6 February the *Navarino* anchored in Port Stanley harbour, and after nearly a year's absence I was back in what I regarded as home. The day was beautiful weatherwise, but my memory of it is clouded by the fact that, when officials arrived on board to clear the vessel, I was handed an immigration notice allowing me to stay for only three months. Further, within ten minutes of landing, I met the manager of the Falkland Islands Company, who handed me a notice ordering me to leave the house I rented from the Company. It was a sad return, and, had I not had so many other things to see to, it would probably have had a very deep effect on me.

More upsets were to come. While talking with a friend, I learned that the Marine Detachment based in the islands had recently held a night exercise on Volunteer Beach, which was well known as the islands' main breeding ground for king penguins. To have used it for such an operation was inexcusable, and showed that wildlife still came very low on the authorities' scale of values. Peter Scott overheard the conversation and said he would inquire further on the matter.

Before we sailed for Carcass Island, which was to be our first port of call for viewing wildlife, I received one more indication that I could expect trouble with my plans. By tradition (some would call it monopoly), the Falkland Islands Company had been the sole agency for ships arriving in the Falklands. However, the Lindblad expeditions had been arranged without reference to the company, and I foresaw that problems would arise when it was discovered I was acting for Lindblad. For some years I had advocated the idea that people should visit the islands to see their wealth of wildlife, but the company had shown no interest. Now that somebody had acted on the idea and shown its economic potential, I suspected that the company would want to jump on the bandwagon. I was not far wrong in this, for on returning to the ship I discovered the company's manager inquiring about the potential of the Lindblad expedition.

At the start I had made it clear to Lindblad Travel that my interest was in conservation, and that, although I would plan their expeditions and show tourists some of the finest wildlife areas in the islands, I would be assisting solely for the sake of the islands' wildlife. If the Falkland Islands Company became involved, conservation would probably become a secondary consideration. In arranging the expeditions I had chosen West Point and Carcass as two of the areas to be visited, both being ideal for wildlife; but my main reason for choosing them was that their owners—Roddy and Lilly Napier and Cecil and Kitty Bertrand—had been allies in the scheme to preserve wildlife and should therefore be the first to benefit from the expeditions.

Annie, who had returned to the Falklands some weeks before me, had gone on ahead to West Point and Carcass to help organise for the Lindblad expedition. After the visit was over, she and I stayed on Carcass for a few days, discussing plans for the future with Cecil and Kitty. We then returned to Stanley. My mind was still on the Volunteer Beach episode, and, although Peter Scott had already mentioned this to the Colonial Secretary, I wrote explaining the situation and enclosing a detailed map showing where all the king penguins in the area were to be found. I gathered that the fact that the matter had been raised through Peter Scott had already earned me the Government's disfavour, and I received proof of this when my map was returned with a curt note. It seemed that I had not made a very good re-entrance into the Falklands.

Back in Stanley, I was faced with the problem of housing. As a Government employee Annie had been allotted a single flat, but for me the situation was more difficult. Fortunately I had some good friends, two of them being Jill and Nigel Miller. Nigel was Captain of the *Darwin*, which plied between Stanley and Montevideo. He and

Jill now came to the rescue by offering me accommodation until I could find a home. I owe them a great deal, for without their assistance I might well have been forced to leave.

Another problem was the immigration order limiting my stay to three months, which, considering that I had already lived and worked in the islands for many years, seemed absurd. I never did discover why officialdom had descended upon me in this manner, but at the time I felt that it had something to do with my strong feelings about conservation. I did not know what the law said about immigration, but naturally assumed that I was on the wrong side. However, on checking the matter, I discovered to my amazement there was no doubt that I did qualify as a resident. I immediately wrote to the Government pointing this out, and heard little more on the matter.

As it was already getting late in the season and many birds were migrating, there was little chance for me to do any fieldwork. Consequently, I devoted myself to writing correspondence, reports and articles and to painting. The arrival of the liner *Sagafiord* in March gave me an opportunity to sell some of my pictures, which, indeed, sold so readily that I began to realise that perhaps I had undervalued them. I took on board a dozen or so paintings, and in next to no time these had gone and I had taken enough orders to keep me busy through the winter months. This certainly was a great help, even if I had underrated my talents!

In mid March I made one short field trip. News reached me that eighteen sperm whales had come ashore on Pleasant Roads, a beach near Fitzroy settlement. Some time earlier I had collected two unusual whales for Dr Fraser of the British Museum, and at the time it seemed a reasonable idea to collect one of these sperm whales. Pleasant Roads beach lay on Falkland Islands Company land, so I asked Mr Young, the manager, whether I might procure one of the skeletons. At first the request was refused, as the company wished to extract and sell the whales' teeth, on which a high value was placed. Nobody, I was told, was allowed on the beach until the teeth had been collected by the company. However, a few days later I heard that the whales were in such a rotten state that nobody wanted the job! Rather amused by this, I went to see Young and offered to do the job on condition that I was allowed one of the skeletons complete with teeth. On 13 March I set off, planning to camp close to the stranded whales until I had completed the job. It was an incredible sight: eighteen creatures forty to fifty feet long, lying side by side along the beach. There had been a very high tide on 14 February, and, as the whales had been discovered shortly after, I suspected that they had come ashore then. All were males and, excepting one old animal, were fairly young. More astonishing was that the old male lay at the head of the line of bodies and appeared to have gone ashore first, as though leading the rest of the pod.

For five days, in some of the most miserable weather I had ever experienced at that time of year, I camped close to the whales. The animals lay half buried in sand, their jaws locked by the terrific weight of their heads. Cutting the teeth out was problem enough, and I could see that saving a skeleton was going to be a hopeless task; they would have to be left for a year or more to allow all the flesh to rot off. The only way that I could get the teeth was by cutting them out in a large piece of flesh. I had often boiled skulls of animals to clear them of flesh, so, on finding an old oil drum on the beach, I cut out the end to make a boiler. Like many Falkland beaches, Pleasant Roads had a good supply of driftwood, so by the second day I had built a small tryworks, and after a short boiling the teeth came away cleanly. It was not hard to imagine how sealers and penguin oilers must have operated. I had guessed that, when these men were boiling down penguins and seal blubber for oil, they had kept their fires going with driftwood and perhaps the animals' carcasses as well. In similar fashion, I found I could keep my fire going with pieces of whale blubber and meat from the boiler, and was able to keep such a good fire that I gave up using my primus and every evening cooked a meal over the hot embers. Fitzroy farm had supplied me with a mutton carcass and potatoes, so on an improvised spit I lived well, off barbecued meat and roast potatoes.

The two whales that I had collected before, a Cuvier's beaked specimen from West Falkland, and a Layard's or strap-toothed whale from quite near where I was now working, were quite rare: indeed, a stranded Layard's whale had apparently been found only once before, in 1877 and, coincidentally, in the same area. Stranded sperm whales are far more common and I expected to find that Dr Fraser already had a specimen. This proved to be the case, and for that I was truly thankful.

In May I received from the publishers David and Charles a letter asking if I would be interested in writing a book about the Falklands.

By the same mail I received two other wonderful pieces of news. Herbert Mills wrote to say that the WWF had approved my project and that I was awarded a grant of £1,000; and news came that Shona and Sharron were to come and join me in the Falklands. I had missed the children immensely, particularly when I heard that Shona was in hospital with a broken leg, having been run over by a car. Fortunately she was now on the mend and both girls would be arriving soon. Irene was remarrying and was taking Alistair to Venezuela.

In July I flew to Carcass by way of the Jasons, combining a seal survey with a visit to Cecil and Kitty Bertrand. Now that the girls were coming to join me, the problem of finding a house had become critical, and I was thinking of following up Kitty's suggestion that I build a house on Carcass. Further, Cecil and Kitty had mentioned to Annie and me that they intended giving up Carcass and thought that we should have the first opportunity of buying it. Carcass Island I considered deserving of protection, and I wondered if I could buy the island with assistance from the WWF and establish and manage it as a reserve.

At about this time the question of Argentina's claim to sovereignty over the Falklands was continually being raised and people felt very uneasy, suspecting that Britain might be thinking of handing over the islands. To the few who knew the Falklands and their way of life, the possibility of this seemed inconceivable; but there is no telling with politicians or governments.

I wondered what the situation would be if there were a change of sovereignty: would the existing reserves and sanctuaries survive? I did not know the answer, but what I had seen of conservation in South America gave me little cause for hope. I was now of the opinion that we should go all out to obtain international recognition of reserves, in order to improve the chances of their being respected.

Some time before the visit to Carcass I had learned that Grand and Steeple Jason Islands were up for sale. Since my first visit there, I had become very attached to them, and saw them as valuable wild-life areas. At the time the idea of attempting to buy them had gone through my mind, but I had given up the thought as ridiculous. Later I began seriously to wonder whether something might be arranged after all and approached Roddy and Lilly Napier and Cecil and Kitty Bertrand with a plan for a joint purchase. If this could be effected and the islands established as reserves through the WWF and IUCN, we could then, I argued, recover our outlay by charging tourist expeditions a landing fee. Nothing came of this proposal, but

Rockhopper Penguins

Adult pair of Rockhopper penguins (*Eudyptes crestatus*) with youngster. Numerous colonies of Rockhoppers, the Islands' smallest breeding penguin, inhabit many coastal regions. In certain areas they form densely populated colonies numbering hundreds of thousands of birds. During the winter these penguins migrate from the Falklands spending some six months at sea, returning to breed at the beginning of the austral summer in October.

I did not give up hope.

Early in August I was given further reason to think that I was right in advocating international reserves. It was announced that, owing to the fact that dairymen in Stanley were short of fodder, the Governor in Council had sanctioned the cutting of tussac grass on Kidney Island, which had been declared a nature reserve only four years before. No doubt areas of tussac could be cut without much damage being done, but the Government owned tussac islands closer to Stanley, and Kidney was, after all, a reserve—an area to be closed and left untouched. I wrote to the Government explaining these points from the conservation angle, and received a lengthy reply stating the problems of maintaining a local supply of milk and that it was not the Government's intention to allow the continued cutting of tussac. According to the letter the decision had not been taken easily; but it had been allowed and so had created a dangerous precedent that augured badly for all other reserves in the islands.

I wrote to Herbert Mills, Kingsland Crowe and Peter Scott on the question of purchasing reserves, pointing out the problems raised by the sovereignty question and outlining my interest in Steeple and Grand Jason and their purchase. I also mentioned my hopes for using wildlife tourism to support conservation projects and that I thought that the Lindblad expeditions might help. Mills said that the WWF had hoped that this travel group would become a supporter of the Fund, but that they had yet to see any substantial support from this source. I wondered about this: clearly Lindblad Travel was a commercial enterprise, but I was sure that it was possible to direct such activities so that they could help conservation.

The idea of tourists coming to the Falklands was still treated sceptically in the islands, even though the *Navarino* visit had been a success. However, attitudes were questioned when, without my knowing, the article that I had written for the *New York Times* was published. This concerned the potential of wildlife tourism in the islands and mentioned that the only way to reach the Falklands from the American continent was by the Falkland Islands Company vessel *Darwin*. Those interested in visiting the islands wrote to the company in Stanley asking for details of passages, and so many letters were received that a duplicated reply had to be printed and sent out. For a long while the company were baffled by this sudden interest, and it was only when someone enclosed a cutting of the article that they realised who was responsible! The manager jumped on me for this, but, as I pointed out, did it not prove something?

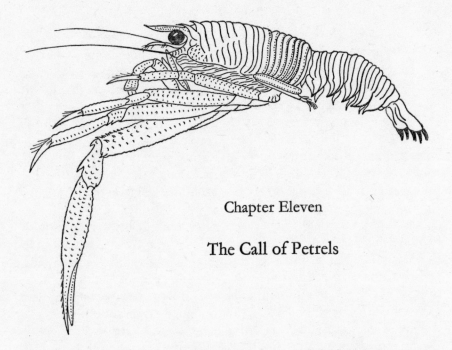

Chapter Eleven

The Call of Petrels

For some years I had had a special interest in Bird Island, which lies
south of Port Stephens in West Falkland. Aerial photographs taken
during the seal survey indicated that the island, which was Government-owned, contained extensive breeding grounds of petrels and
other species, and was generally in good condition. On checking
back, I found no record that the island had ever been stocked with
sheep or cattle, though it had been worked by fur sealers. All this
suggested that the island could and should be made a reserve; but,
though I twice recommended that this be done, little interest was
shown in the suggestion.

Bird was not as remote as many offshore islands, but the fact that
little shipping passed the island made it by no means easy to reach.
Several times I thought of the possibility of using the Beaver float
plane, and during aerial surveys both Jim and Ian (the pilots) had
indicated that in perfect conditions the aircraft could probably land
close to the island. The biggest problem would be getting from the
aircraft to dry land, as there were no beaches that the Beaver could
safely approach, and I suspected that, even if it could be brought
within a few yards of the shoreline, deep water would prevent wad-
ing ashore. I wondered about using a wet suit, but there remained the
problem of landing equipment. The best plan seemed to be to use a
small inflatable dinghy.

Accordingly, in November 1968, shortly before the petrel breeding season began, I made final plans and put the idea to Jim Kerr, Superintendent of Civil Aviation. I think the idea appealed to him, and, though he was a little concerned about sea conditions off Bird Island, he was prepared to make the attempt.

The Government agreed to the visit provided that I took the required safety precautions—that is, took someone along and made sure of taking a radio transmitter. Getting someone to join me was again a problem, but finally Ian Monkman, who worked for the European Space Research Organisation's local establishment, agreed to come.

The flight was made on 3 December 1968, a brilliant day with excellent visibility and a light wind. On the way out we passed over the Arch Islands, a small group of tussac-covered islands lying close to Port Albemarle on West Falkland. Against the deep buffs, browns and sober greens of the mainland, these tiny islands showed green and alive, giving point to their value as tussac reserves.

From the Arch Islands we passed over Cape Meredith on West Falkland and then were in sight of Bird Island, which is roughly triangular with three dome-shaped points. Most of the island was thickly covered with tussac, but in the centre, where the ground was lower, was a small pond at one end of which was an area clear of vegetation and suitable for camping.

Jim decided to take a closer look at the water and approached an area where he thought a landing could be made. We moved in low towards the cliffs, obtaining our first impression of just how formidable the coast was; but, when we were just a few feet off the surface, Jim suddenly took the aircraft into a tight turn and up again, saying that he did not like the look of the swell. I think he must have seen the disappointment written in my face, for almost directly he turned again, to take another look. This time we went further in and, with the cliffs looming up before us, touched down. I cannot remember how many times we bounced on the waves before we came to rest, but the feeling was by no means pleasant. As we sat going gently up and down with the swell, there was silence. Then Jim exclaimed, "Well, you're here at last, but I don't know how you're going to get off again, for I'm bloody well not coming to get you!"

However, leaving was the last of my worries at that moment: I was too concerned with the problems of getting ashore. The beach where we hoped to land lay about 150 yards away, at the head of a slightly curving bay flanked with towering cliffs and leading directly

THE CALL OF PETRELS

into a long valley. The scene was one of breathtaking beauty, but awesome, and I had the feeling of being very small and insignificant.

The whole bay was alive with the sound of birds, with groups of penguins porpoising about the water. The swell was gentle, but strong enough to make it difficult to keep balance; and, while pumping out the dinghy—a job that had to be done outside the plane, on one of its floats—I had to keep an arm crooked round one of the struts. Eventually the job was done and I began loading the dinghy for the first of three trips ashore.

From our position it was impossible to tell what landing would be like. I could hear the waves breaking on the beach, and estimated that there was about two feet of swell. Venturing out, I looked down into the sea: it was a fantastic colour and so clear that it was possible to see through about six fathoms of water.

Sixty yards from the beach was a thick belt of kelp. This in itself was no problem, for the dinghy slid over it easily; but halfway across it I heard a crash of water and, on looking round, saw a group of sealion plunging into the sea and swimming towards me. I was not particularly concerned, for they would not molest me intentionally, but not being used to humans they would probably be inquisitive. Soon they were all around me, diving under the boat and emerging inches away from the oars. However, after an initial inspection they kept their distance and I reached the shore without mishap.

The beach was made up of large, rounded boulders, and, as the tide was low, there was the problem of keeping a footing on boulders covered with seaweed. The swell appeared low, but when the boat was right in I realised just how tiny a bundle of rubber it was and had to jump for the shore in order to stop the dinghy from being swamped. Fortunately, although I was wet and found it difficult to keep my balance, I managed to keep the equipment dry.

Half an hour later, Ian and I and all our equipment were ashore and the Beaver was preparing for take-off. Jim now had an aircraft clear of passengers and cargo, and therefore could take off with a short run—so avoiding the need to go round to the lee of the island and into rougher waters. Even so, the swell was such that, from where we were standing, the floats kept disappearing from view. As the plane took off over the beach, through the valley and away, I thought of Jim's remark and wondered if he would come back to fetch us!

We were only about 200 yards from our proposed camp site, but the intervening tussac was so thick and the ground so rough that it took us two hours to get all our equipment there. The position, however, was ideal, with a beautiful view down to the opposite shoreline, where immense cliffs plunged sheer to the sea. The calls of fur seal could be heard, appearing to issue from fissures in the cliffs, but no fur seal could be seen. As we had flown over the island I had noticed that in certain places the grass appeared to follow distinct lines, like geological faults. Later we realised the importance of these peculiarities in the tussac growth; had we not, we might never have left the island.

We had brought a small supply of water with us, for from the air the pond had looked shallow and rather muddy. On inspection, it was found to be almost stagnant. Close by, formed from the outflow from the pond, was a smaller and cleaner-looking pool. However, owing to the fact that rockhopper penguins washed there after leaving the sea, it tasted very salty and was not suitable for drinking. This left us with the four gallons we had brought with us, and, as we were to be on the island for at least a fortnight, we had to ration ourselves severely.

Petrels' nesting holes were everywhere, and many of the tussac stools were peppered with them. About the tent were numerous slabs of rock, and beneath every one there were signs of excavation. The evidence suggested that these burrows belonged to prions and diving petrels, but nightfall would bring the proof.

Our Arctic Guinea tent was large enough for the two of us and some equipment, but could not accommodate our food stocks, cooking equipment and stove. Using a small tarpaulin that I always took about with me, and supporting the upturned dinghy on four conveniently placed tussac stools, we formed a second shelter. Under this rather rough cover, we stored the rest of our equipment and did our cooking.

We could still hear the calls of fur seal but had yet to see one. Most of the sounds seemed to be coming from the cliffs close to where I had noted the faults in the ground. At one point we discovered a small group of fur seal tucked beneath overhangs in the cliff face, perhaps 100 feet below us; but, as we moved inland we could still hear seal, whose calls appeared to be coming from inland of our position. The shape of the island lent itself to echo, so I put it down to this. Fifty yards inland, and in line with a deep fissure in the cliff edge, we came across a number of hollows in the ground.

Suddenly it came to me that the odd line that I had noted in the tussac growth did in fact mark a geological fault and that we were walking over a crack in the island. The calls of seal could still be heard, and so could the soft murmur of surf. We now took great care where we walked and were glad we did so, for further on we came across a narrow gap from which issued the sounds of seal and of the sea far below. The fissure must have run right across the island, and, though it was mostly covered, like a crevasse covered with snow, it was here and there exposed. Probably the seal calls we heard were echoes, but it is possible that some seal had travelled along the fissure. More fissures were found, and, as it was impossible to determine exactly how well they were covered, we decided to keep away from this area altogether.

In all, we had seen thirty adult seal and six pups. This was interesting, for, in sailing round the island in 1951, Dr Richard Laws had found one colony of about thirty animals. This provided further support for my findings that the fur seal population of the Falklands had remained fairly static since then.

Our first night on Bird Island turned out to be another memorable experience. Though it had been my intention to stay up to see what petrels were breeding on the island, we were both so tired that we decided to get a good night's sleep and stay up the following evening. We slept until nearly midnight, but not after that! Suddenly I was woken by objects sliding down the tent. Then I was conscious of the most weird cacophony of sound. I had heard prions and diving petrels before, but not in such numbers. Above these calls I could pick out the sound of wing beats—very fast, almost furious —then a splash or thump as a petrel landed close by. Now and again there would be a thud on the tent, and a petrel would slide down the side. Outside the din was increasing as more and more birds arrived and sought their burrows, and eventually the sound was like that of some great waterfall. This echoed back and forth across the valley, a sound not to be forgotten. Gone was our sleep, and not until about four in the morning, when the birds started to leave again for the sea, did we get any further rest.

I had hoped to find a lot of Johnny Rooks on the island, but on first inspection I began to wonder if any would be discovered. On other islands they immediately made their presence known, yet that had not happened here. A day or two after our arrival I noticed an adult pair nesting no distance from our camp. What puzzled me was that they hardly moved, and for most of the day appeared to be

asleep, which was odd indeed. One evening I climbed to the top of
a hill to see if the prions formed rafts on the water before they
started their flight in; and, just before the light finally failed, a
number of Johnny Rooks flew over and settled in various areas of
the tussac. They sat quietly about until the prions appeared sweeping
through the sky; then, coming to life, they started to dive about,
hunting in the tussac. Obviously these Johnny Rooks lived largely
off the petrels and to do so had turned semi-nocturnal.

Like all the islands I had visited, Bird had its own characteristics.
Much of the rock was a beautiful reddy-pink colour and similar to
sandstone. The whole island appeared to be built up of horizontal
layers of these sedimentary rocks, with softer layers having formed
between harder ones. Through time some of the soft layers had been
etched away, producing not only numerous undercut cliffs and deep
shelving, but also a most peculiar formation of small stalagmites.
Close to our camp site were huge slabs of rock with these small
formations all over them, the likes of which I had yet to see anywhere else in the Falklands. At Port Stephens I had seen what was
called the Indian Village—a vast collection of stacks, buttresses and
outcrops of rock on the top of a hill. From a distance this formation
had the appearance of a camp site—hence its name. On Bird Island
was a similar formation: the top of one of the hills appeared from a
distance to be cut square, while the rest of the hill was dome-shaped.
The whole area was thickly covered in tussac, so it was difficult to
make out the actual formation. Making the climb up this hill, we
were surprised to discover that the top was made up of several huge
square-cut outcrops, perhaps twenty feet high, with wide fissures
running between them and joining to form a sun trap at the centre.
It was a windy day, but there an eerie calm prevailed and the
temperature caused us to sweat under our anoraks.

On our fourth day on Bird Island our water problem was overcome through a sudden deluge of rain. A spare blanket we were
using over the sleeping bags at night was quickly brought into
service and used to collect rainwater, and by this means we managed
to fill up all our spare containers.

The next day we woke to find it very cold, overcast, and with a
fair wind from the west. Throughout the day the weather deterio-
rated, until the wind reached gale force. The tent was now suffering
from a side wind and we were continually having to fasten the pegs,
which kept pulling out of the soft peaty ground. The makeshift
shelter was affected even more, with the dinghy in danger of being

A reconstruction of the sealing and penguin oiling try-pot
and lances found on Bird Island

blown away; so we were forced to take the lot down and stow everything under the boat. It was now raining again and the pond level was rising. Before the day was out the tent was an island, and though the surrounding water was only two or three inches deep, it seemed that we would soon have to move. This would by no means have been easy, as there was no other clear ground, but fortunately the water level remained as it was, even though the rain continued for another two days. By this time the guys on one side of the tent were chaffed through by continual movement, and we prevented further damage only by taking large tussac stools and stacking them to the windward side, to give extra shelter. On Tuesday morning the wind abated, leaving thick damp cloud hanging over the island. Everything looked grey, felt damp and made us feel miserable. For two days we had been unable to cook, having subsisted on cold food and the occasional hot drink prepared in the tent.

We had last spoken to Stanley four days before, so, now that the weather was clearing, the transmitter was unwrapped and a message sent saying that, though wet, we were fine. Anxious to get some exercise, we set off for an area we had not yet visited. About half an hour later we heard a Beaver approaching. It was then that I realised that a few days earlier we had asked for a new supply of batteries to be dropped. Though we felt very conspicuous and the plane flew right over us, we were not spotted, and we could not tell whether anything had been dropped. A long search revealed nothing, and it seemed that the parcel, if it had been dropped, was lost in the tussac. The following day we heard from Stanley that the pilot had dropped the parcel, and that he thought it had landed close to the tent; but still we could find nothing. It was not until the next day, when the weather was drier and I decided to repitch the tent, that the batteries were found: right underneath the side flaps of the tent!

The black-browed albatross were now hatching their eggs, and as a result there was a great deal of activity as birds flew to and from their nests, feeding their young. This gave me the opportunity to film, from close to, these birds in flight. As I watched them I noticed that when the wind was in a certain direction large numbers would fly along the cliff to a rocky ledge, over which they would effortlessly soar. For hours I sat on that ledge, watching and filming those masters of flight as they approached and rose above me, using hardly a wing beat and riding the currents of air. Yet on land these birds were the clumsiest creatures, expending enormous amounts of energy in the effort of walking about their colonies.

For a few days the weather remained bright, but on 13 December conditions changed to bring another dull, cloudy day with a cool wind. Gradually the wind increased to such a force that clouds of spray showered the island, coating our tent with salt. This was a nuisance, for, until the tent got a good hard rain on it again, the cloth would remain sticky and damp. For the next few days the sea on the east side of the island was spectacular, with huge waves churning up the bay and breaking on the shore.

With hatching well under way, large numbers of rockhopper penguins were coming to the island. The roughness of the sea and the coastline did not deter them, and with amazing resilience they withstood a battering so fierce that it would have smashed any boat to pulp in a few minutes. The huge breakers literally threw the birds on the rocks; then, before they could pick themselves up, sucked them back and threw them down again. Watching this, one would have imagined the death toll to be tremendous; yet only once did I come across a bird that might have received injuries from its batterings. Giant petrels and sealion were more of a problem, and would lie offshore, just out of the surf, and prey on birds that were tiring of their efforts to swim against such seas. However, even these predators were not immune from difficulties, and one sealion I saw trying to catch penguins had to give up from exhaustion.

I had hoped to find a lot of sealion on Bird Island, but was disappointed. Only forty were found, even though the island had once supported large herds. This was shown by the areas of tussac peat that had been smoothed down by these animals and become dark and stained, with an almost polished surface. Tussac stools had been worn and deep channels had been formed between the growths. These areas took an amazingly long time to revert to their original state, and it was only after many years that the vegetation that normally grows under tussac canopies would begin to reappear. Owing to this, areas that appeared to have been used by seal until very recently had in fact been deserted long before, even though old seal skeletons still lay exposed on the surface.

A complaint often made by farmers was that the Magellan penguin and thin-billed prion caused soil erosion. I argued that overgrazing was mainly to blame, and that, if grazing were controlled, soil erosion would be greatly reduced, and the birds would actually assist the farmer by supplying nutrients to the grasses about their burrows. Bird Island provided impressive evidence of the point I was trying to make.

On some of the sharper slopes on the island, there were large colonies of thin-billed prions; and, as we crossed these areas, our feet would be continually breaking through the peaty ground and into the prions' burrows. The prions' burrowing activities had given the ground the appearance of having been tilled, and the tussac growth thereabouts was some of the richest I have seen. Instead of growing from individual stools, the grass appeared to sprout all over, giving an almost complete cover. Thus, though the slopes were exposed and the earth soft and crumbly, the soil was held together and protected from erosion by the tussac, the luxuriant growth of which was directly attributable to the prions' burrowings and the nutrients supplied by the birds' droppings. The birds were not assisting, but helping to prevent, erosion, which otherwise would probably have been severe.

In a small bay below one of the main rookeries of black-browed albatross and rockhopper penguins, I came across signs of penguin oilers' workings. On flat shelving rocks was a corral with dry stone walling, and on the rocks the claw marks of penguins could be seen, showing a route by which these birds had once made their way to the rookery. Obviously, the penguin oilers had built their corral where they could round up the birds as they came ashore; but less obvious was where the birds had been rendered down, as there was little room nearby for firing try pots. However, just below was a perfectly formed natural quay where a schooner could have moored and where the slaughtered birds could have been loaded without difficulty. I wondered if the try pots had been fired on board the ship.

On our last day on the island I came across an encampment that might have been used by sealers. As we were bringing our equipment down to the bay where we had landed, I discovered a try pot among the boulders on the beach. One side was broken, but the pot had clearly been about four feet in diameter and twenty-odd inches deep, and was similar in type to the try pots I had seen on Grand Jason. Further inland there were signs of habitation, and protruding from the peat was the square metal shaft of a sealing lance with a spade-shaped end.

In the same area I unearthed a hand-made leather sandal of a style worn about a century ago, and found pieces of ship timber, a sheet of lead and, the most exciting find, an old bottle, which had been kept in perfect condition by the peat. It was made of a lovely green-brown shade of glass and was the first such bottle that I had ever found complete. Some years later I discovered that this particular type of bottle had been used over a century ago by a Dutch firm of gin producers.

This happy find helped to make our last day on Bird Island something special. The day was hot and calm, and conditions were favourable fot the Beaver to collect us. Communications had not been good during the past few days, so we were not sure exactly when we would be collected, and by early evening were wondering if we would be! However, Ian Campbell, who was our pilot for the flight back, had deliberately left his arrival late, expecting conditions to be best later in the day.

As we stood on the floats of the plane, having a last look at the bay, I felt sorry to be leaving, though I was nonetheless looking forward to getting home. I was not quite sure what my companion Ian thought, and wondered if he had found his stay on the island too much. Apparently this was far from being the case, though it was only after he had been killed in a road accident in Stanley that I discovered the truth of the matter. His mother visited the Falklands after his death, and from her I learned that he had rated his stay on Bird Island as one of the greatest experiences in his life.

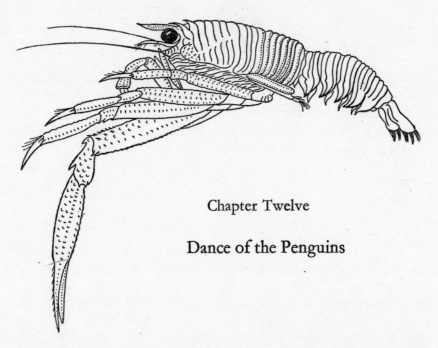

Chapter Twelve

Dance of the Penguins

It was now almost six months since Shona and Sharron had arrived. We now felt more like a family, although the accommodation problem was still not settled. In an effort to obtain more security, Annie and I decided to get married; and, since we had no wish to do this in Stanley, we arranged for our marriage to take place on West Point, with Roddy acting as officiary. The wedding was fixed for mid January, at about the same time as another Lindblad expedition was expected; so, in order to organise for both, Annie and the girls went on ahead of me to West Point, while I stayed in Stanley to await the expedition.

As I had a few days to spare before the expedition was due, I decided to travel to Volunteer Point, on the north coast, to check on the king penguin colony. This I found was progressing well, and comprised twenty adult birds, all sitting on eggs or with young. I was greatly encouraged by this, and felt that, if the birds could be looked after for a few more years, they would have established a substantial rookery.

Back in Stanley I received conflicting reports about the expedition vessel. Lindblad had chartered an Argentine boat, the *Aquiles*, and it began to seem doubtful whether she would call at the Falklands as planned. A day or two before her due date of arrival, I heard that she would not be calling after all, no doubt because of the difficulties of political relations between Argentina and the Falklands. It was a blow, as I was hoping again to demonstrate the strength of outside interest in the islands' wildlife.

Annie and I were married on 18 January 1969, with only Roddy's family, Shona and Sharron, and two close friends, Maureen and Geoff Douglas, in attendance. Looking back, I think that I must have been the worst groom ever; certainly there cannot have been many grooms who have insisted on taking their own wedding photographs! Apart from this, however, I spent the day fairly conventionally, though it was not long before I was back to my usual activities.

When the Reserves and Sanctuaries Ordinance had been enacted, Roddy had agreed to let two of his small islands, Low Island and Dunbar Island, become sanctuaries. These and the Twins, two islets belonging to Kitty and Cecil Bertrand, became the first privately owned islands to come under the new order. From aerial surveys I knew a little of Low and Dunbar, but I had never landed on them. It was therefore arranged that we should visit them during our stay on West Point.

Although it had been declared a sanctuary, Dunbar still supported sheep, which had completely eaten away the tussac on what had once been a rich tussac island. Some 300 sheep had been on this 590-acre island for ten years, and, though Roddy intended removing them, I believe that he felt he was too late. He admitted that the bird life had dropped off and that some seal colonies had vanished, but he had been forced to consider first the economics of stocking the island. Erosion had yet to set in and there was hope that the tussac would re-establish itself, as the old stools remained and there was a chance that some seed was lying dormant; but there was less hope that the island's bird and animal life would become as before.

On Low Island the situation was completely different. A few cattle grazed there, but had made little difference to the tussac. Cattle, being rough grazers, would feed off the coarser parts of the tussac, so having little effect on its growth; but sheep would go for the more succulent centre growth, thereby causing the eventual death of the plant.

Although I deplored the system of stocking offshore tussac islands, and held it responsible for unnecessary destruction of this grass, I believed that much of the original tussac had been destroyed

Night Heron

Night Heron (*Nycticorax n. cyanocephalus*) in adult plumage, a contrast to the rather sober buffs and browns of the immatures. The species is found fairly commonly in many coastal areas of the Falklands where it generally nests in the shelter of tussac grass growing on rocky coastal faces. Night Herons feed on small fish, usually on an incoming tide. Their stealth, patience and dexterity are quite an interesting study in themselves.

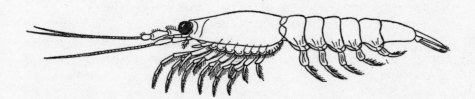

A form of "krill" or whale food on which many species of penguin
subsist. This is a species of Euphausian.

long ago and in other ways. During the early period of settlement, a lot of tussac was fired in order to get at seal or drive out the pigs that had been introduced to provide a ready supply of meat. Large herds of pigs roamed freely on many islands, and they alone must have destroyed vast areas of tussac. Later, on New Island, I saw the damage that pigs could do to colonies of prions, and so formed the opinion that these animals must have been responsible not only for destroying a great deal of tussac, but also for causing the disappearance of many colonies of ground-nesting petrels.

While camping on Low Island, I was awoken early one morning by Magellan penguins calling close by. On the beach were five or six birds arranged in a circle and slowly moving around together, raising and lowering their heads. This was the first time I had seen at such close quarters this unusual penguin dance. Now and again the group would call out, and then, for no apparent reason, break formation and rush into the sea, only to return minutes later and repeat the display. This went on for about twenty minutes, after which it was brought to an abrupt conclusion by the appearance of an old bull sealion. The birds scattered into the sea and away, but still the seal made a half-hearted charge in pursuit of them.

Seeing the tremendous bulk of these aged male seal, it is not easy to imagine them capable of catching the much smaller and swifter penguins, but I had often seen it happen. Frequently the seal would lie, apparently asleep, in a place that the penguins would pass on their way from the sea to the tussac. When a penguin came close, the seal would suddenly lift himself and charge for the sea, correctly anticipating that the penguin would do likewise. In the water, the penguins, for some unexplained reason, invariably chose to swim in a circle rather than directly out to sea, and so were often caught within seconds of entering the water. Bringing his victim to the surface, the seal would then slap the bird back and forth on the water. When he had done this five or six times, the body would be completely stripped of its skin. Yet often the seal would not eat his victim, but simply toss it aside and return again to the beach. Most puzzling to me was the fact that it was almost always solitary old bulls that killed penguins in this way. Only once did I see more than one seal involved, and then the killing was done by the adult bull.

Arrangements had been made to pick us up from Low Island on the last day of January. When Roddy arrived in *Gleam* from West Point, a fair wind was blowing and it was essential to leave directly, in case conditions became much worse. However, in anchoring,

Gleam's prop became fouled with the kedge anchor rope, and, as we had no time to try and clear the prop, we had to cut it. Because of this we could not use the engine and had to make the voyage under sail.

No sooner were we clear of Low Island than the wind increased suddenly from twenty to fifty or more knots. A strong tide ran between Low Island and the Sound, and, though the entrance to the Sound lay only a mile or two away, to reach it took us an hour and a half of battling against the wind and tide. Once we were in the Sound, *Gleam* showed how she could sail and ploughed swiftly ahead; but, with the wind coming on us so violently and the sea throwing us about, we found it impossible to get another reef in the sail. All we could do was hope that nothing carried away. Maureen, Geoff and Sharron were below deck, and, when I checked to see that they were all right, I found water everywhere and Maureen's face green with fear. The water puzzled me, for normally the boat kept fairly dry below; but, as the vessel heeled over, a jet of water shot from below the decking at a point where I had earlier been carrying out repairs and had taken out a bolt that went through the hull. The hole had been plugged, but the force of water outside had pushed out the plug. Maureen's fears came partly from the sight of so much water washing around, and partly from overhearing a conversation in the wheelhouse. Several times we had said "She's not going to make it", meaning that the boat would not clear a certain point at one tack. Maureen, however, had taken the remark to mean that the boat was doomed.

As we went up the Sound the wind reached its maximum and every bit of rigging was straining. Suddenly there was a report like a rifle shot as one of the wire stays on the port side snapped like string. We could only hope that no more went, for the masthead was already under tremendous strain. Yet shortly afterwards another stay snapped, and, though it was only a back stay this time, this further weakened the mast. Fortunately we were now able to get out of the worst of the wind by running close to West Falkland, on the last stretch of our journey to West Point. By this means we were able to reach shelter safely, after an adventure that none of us wanted to repeat.

Towards the end of February I received from various settlements reports that large numbers of Gentoo penguins were being found dead in their rookeries. From some specimens flown in at my request, I discovered that these were young birds hatched that season, and that all of them were rather thin, with empty stomachs. It was impossible for me to tell exactly why this was so, but I strongly suspected that it was the indirect result of egg collecting. The breeding cycle of these penguins is quite regular and fits in with the related food chains. Each season at a precise time, the birds arrive to breed, and egg laying, hatching and the rearing of the young all take place in accord with a strict timetable. But what happens if the cycle is disrupted by egg collecting? Normally, Gentoo, Magellan and rockhopper penguin eggs are collected under licence, and collectors are required by law to take eggs before a certain date. In practice this is impossible to enforce and eggs are sometimes collected later. When the birds lose their first egg they normally lay again, resulting in later hatching; and, where eggs are collected late, hatching may be very late indeed—dangerously so.

When the adult birds are in the final stages of feeding their young, which by then are almost full grown, the amount of krill in Falkland waters is at its greatest. This extra food appears to play a significant part in the final stages of the young birds' growth and may also play a part in inducing these birds to leave the rookeries and fend for themselves. It is possible that young that have hatched very late miss this "flush"; or it may well be that the adult birds, knowing the season is late, leave the rookeries while these young still require feeding. Either way, the youngsters die of starvation.

The collecting of wild-bird eggs that are considered edible is a fairly well established pursuit in the Falklands, where it has long been a tradition. It began in the early days of settlement, and I have spoken to numerous people who can still remember vessels returning to Stanley with their holds full of loosely stored eggs. This no longer happens, but between 1965 and 1970 an average of thirty-three licences for egg collecting were taken out each season, representing 40,000 eggs per year. Egg collecting carried out with due regard for the continued survival of the rookeries is something that I have never been against, and when certain landowners said that Magellan penguins were causing excessive soil erosion and that their colonies ought to be destroyed, I suggested that the owners could gain commercially from the birds' presence if a system for collecting and exporting limited numbers of Magellan eggs were put into effect. I hoped that, if this were done and the owners began to realise the birds' value, they would become inclined to fight soil erosion by replanting tussac, not by destroying penguins.

Generally, I believe, owners are becoming increasingly aware of the need to be more conservative about collecting. Many recognise the value of Gentoo penguins, whose nesting habits help to break down areas of rough pasture, which afterwards become much richer. In some cases farmers entirely prohibit the collection of eggs from their land, so that the Gentoo can multiply and extend its good work.

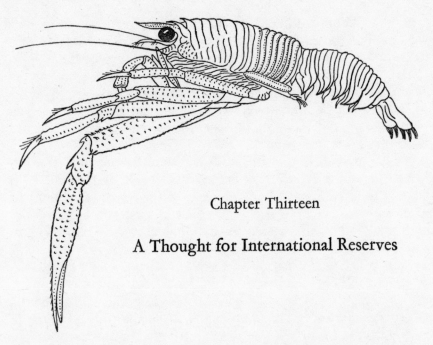

Chapter Thirteen

A Thought for International Reserves

Housing continued to be a problem. In May 1969 we managed to
rent a small and very draughty place at the top end of Port Stanley,
but, though this meant that Annie, the girls and I could all live
under one roof, the place had many drawbacks, such as very
little room for working and no good source of daylight by
which to paint. I started work on the book I had been asked to
write about the Falklands; but in August, by which time I was
progressing well, we received notice from our landlord, who
wished to sell the house. Fortunately we had six months to find
somewhere else, but this nonetheless meant further upheaval and
disruption.

In addition to these domestic problems, I was still very concerned
about the future of Steeple and Grand Jason, which were still on the
open market. I had written to various people—notably Peter Scott,
Kingsland Crowe and Herbert Mills—suggesting that the islands
should be bought as reserves, and had myself considered whether it
would be possible to organise a private joint purchase. However, it
seemed impossible to raise in the Falklands themselves the £10,000
required, so I looked elsewhere for possible sources of finance. I had
assembled quite a large file on the islands, and sent this and many
photographs to Herbert Mills at the WWF in Washington. Mean-
while I had long discussions with Mr A. G. Barton, who, as a

director of Dean Brothers (owners of the two islands in question), was handling the sale. I think he appreciated the effort I was making to find a buyer, and certainly he knew my fondness for the islands. Early on, he offered me first refusal, but I could see no way of getting the purchase price together, other than with outside help. Mr Barton was even prepared to let Steeple Jason go for £3,000 so long as I agreed to rent Grand Jason for ten years; but still I could not find the necessary funds.

My communications with the WWF involved not only Herbert Mills but also Dr Vollmar, Secretary General of the WWF in Switzerland, who on 5 March wrote encouraging me to submit an application for a grant. I had already been discussing this possibility with the WWF's American organisation, and now began to realise that my appeal to Washington was not known in Switzerland. This was confirmed when, in June, Dr Vollmar wrote to me from Rome, where the WWF Conservation Committee had just met and the matter of the two islands had been raised. He asked me to submit a project description. To add to my anxiety there was the problem of having mail only once a month, which meant that obtaining a reply to a letter could take two or even three months.

In February I had written about filming to Len Hill in England and, as an afterthought and rather in jest, had asked him if he were interested in buying a couple of the Jason Islands. On 20 February Len wrote back, "Jason Island. This sounds interesting. What is the price? Could you give me more information?" I sent him more details, and in June read a newspaper article referring to the islands and saying that Len was interested in obtaining them. As it was important to know what was happening, I rang through to England and spoke to Len, who said that he had spoken to Christopher Cadbury of the Society for the Promotion of Nature Reserves about raising the necessary finance.

Immediately after the phone call I wrote again, giving Len more details about Steeple and Grand Jason and sending him a batch of slides and some film of the islands. At the same time I asked Mr Barton if he would hold the sale, as it now looked as though the money could be found.

August 1969 therefore became quite a landmark for me, as it seemed that Steeple and Grand Jason would at last become wildlife reserves. However, I was a little concerned about what Len wanted to do with the islands, as from his later correspondence it appeared that he wished to buy them privately, rather than in co-operation with a conservation body. Still, I had no fears, as I knew Len's interest in conservation.

During the second week in September I made another visit to Volunteer Point, the area of which is one of the Magellan penguin's largest breeding grounds in the Falklands. Every year, many thousands of these birds return from the warmer waters further north to nest in the Volunteer area, and this time I hoped to be there for the first arrivals. I discovered the first Magellan on 13 September, and already it was cleaning out a nest burrow. The following day I watched a second Magellan come ashore with two Gentoo penguins; and later three more Magellans came ashore together. One of these behaved extremely positively, and, after crossing the wide sandy beach to the "greens", where hundreds of burrows were in evidence, made his way to a rise in the ground. There he stopped momentarily, then made an abrupt turn and without further hesitation hurried off down the slope and straight into a burrow. This, of course, was no proof that he had gone to the same burrow as he had used the previous season, but it was remarkable how positive the bird had been in choosing one burrow out of many hundreds. A few days later there were hundreds of Magellans ashore, all, so far as I could see, having arrived individually or in groups of two or three.

When the French first settled the Falklands, in 1764, they brought with them cattle that they had purchased in Montevideo and that probably came from originally Spanish stock. These cattle, which had immense foreshoulders, a short neck, and a powerful head with formidable horns, did well and in a relatively short space of time were quite prolific in the east Falklands. When the islands were deserted, the cattle went wild, and survived well until the British settlement began. In the following half century they were hunted to extinction, or so it was thought, for on Volunteer Point a small herd of distinctively Spanish type remain. Osmund Smith, the owner of the Volunteer area, told me that these cattle had been there for as long as the farm, and that he, like his ancestors, wished to leave them in peace. Though they are not indigenous to the Falklands, the cattle are a piece of living history and of undeniable interest.

While at Volunteer Point, I hoped to see the herd, but all I found was one lone bull, whom I thought it better to leave to himself. I later learned that normally these animals are quite nervous and keep well out of the way, but they are nonetheless deserving of respect.

At the far end of the Point, a sand bar protrudes at right angles to the coast. I had once discovered a solitary king penguin there, and wondered whether a small breeding group had now established itself on the bar. In fact I found four chicks there, representing a small but important increase in the king penguin population, and providing proof that another small colony had been established, in a place that was out of the way for visitors. This latter fact was of great importance, as I found it difficult to make people understand that, although the birds appeared to be tame, they could not, while incubating, tolerate a lot of close approaches, which would eventually cause them to abandon their eggs.

For many years the colony had been a fairly well-kept secret, but after a visit there the Swedish wildlife photographer Sven Gillsater unthinkingly advertised the birds' existence. Before long, people were making the journey to see the penguins, and all I could do was make a point of seeing intending visitors and explaining to them that the birds they would be seeing represented 90 per cent of the total king penguin population of the Falklands and must be treated carefully. Generally visitors did take care, but unfortunately there were exceptions. When, the following March, I visited the colony with Sir Michael Hadow, a keen bird man and then British Ambassador to Argentina, seven abandoned king penguin eggs were discovered round the perimeter of the colony. They appeared to have been abandoned several weeks before, at about the time when the rookery had had a large number of visitors.

On my return to Stanley I found no positive news from Len Hill about whether he was going to buy Steeple and Grand Jason, but I did find a letter from Dr Vollmar, who said that he would contact Peter Scott and ask if he could get in touch with Hill to see whether the islands could be purchased jointly.

Bird Island had now become a wildlife reserve, and Dr Vollmar passed on to me the congratulations of the WWF. My job had been made easier by the fact that the Government was now showing a more sympathetic attitude towards the establishment of reserves and sanctuaries, and by the fact that there was now a new Colonial Secretary, John Jones, who showed a willingness to discuss conservation matters. I had already received a most encouraging letter from the Governor and Colonial Secretary, thanking me for the work I had done in obtaining information on Bird Island.

Replying to Dr Vollmar, I said that it would be excellent if the WWF could have a joint interest in Steeple and Grand Jason. The uncertain political situation was high in my thoughts, as I realised that, if the Falklands were handed over to Argentina, the reserves that were being established would have a much better chance of surviving unviolated if international organisations such as the WWF or IUCN had an interest in them. Then any violators would have more than just a few local conservationists to face.

I was amused to learn that a farm manager had been heard to say over dinner in Stanley that, "at the rate Strange is going on, he will have the whole Falklands made into a bloody wildlife reserve". If I had been there, my answer would simply have been "Why not?" Perhaps I was thinking of just that: making the whole of the Falklands an international reserve. Could it not solve the sovereignty question? There was no reason why, if the islands were made a reserve, sheep farming could not continue; certain areas would have special protection, and restrictions could be imposed on egg collecting, shooting and so on, affecting just a few individuals. The islands would receive tremendous publicity, and wildlife tourism would be greatly enhanced. Naturally I was under no illusion that this was more than a pipedream, knowing full well that the sheep farming community would have none of it.

A great deal of interest was being taken in the immense kelp beds surrounding the Falkland coasts. The species *Macrocystis*, which grew off the Falklands, was already the basis of a large industry in California, where it was processed and sodium alginate extracted. During my stay in California, I had learned a little about how the industry operated, and of the conservation problems associated with the cutting. These were small, provided certain precautions were taken.

In May I had met Michael Perry of the British company Alginate Industries Ltd. He had been on a short fact-finding tour for his company, which was interested in harvesting kelp in the Falklands. As a great deal of wildlife relied on the kelp beds for feed and protection, I approached Mr Perry on the matter, telling him, for instance, of the way the large kelp bed to the northeast of Volunteer Rocks acted as a wave buffer and prevented the sea from washing over the fur seal colony there. A similar situation prevailed in other places, and there was also the possibility that large-scale harvesting of kelp would cause a great increase in coastal erosion. To all these problems I found Mr Perry sympathetic. In a letter to me he stated, "I think that the amount of kelp we shall be harvesting within the next decade is unlikely to have any effect on wildlife, but we shall of course need your suggestions, provided that you do not wish to preserve *all* the kelp within easy reach of Stanley!"

I wrote to Dr Vollmar about the interest being taken in the kelp beds, and said that I was sure that the new industry would co-operate. In addition, the industry was likely to add greatly to our knowledge of the beds and of their biological make-up.

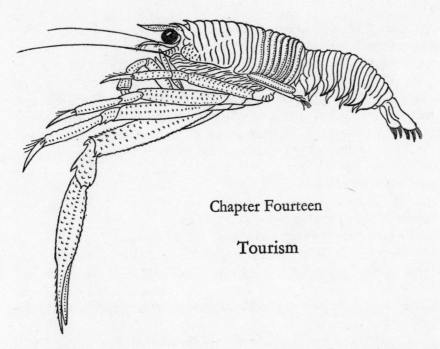

Chapter Fourteen

Tourism

From the beginning of my involvement with Lindblad Travel, I had made it clear to Lars Lindblad that my interest in conservation came first. As Lindblad Travel was primarily a commercial enterprise, it was almost inevitable that there would at some time be a clash of interests, as indeed proved to be the case. Through my articles Lars had learned something of Beauchêne Island and of its vast colony of black-browed albatross, and he asked me if it would be possible to land on the island. I was firmly against the idea, as Beauchêne was an untouched, ecologically perfect island, and to have eighty or ninety people wandering over it would mean disaster. Besides, the island was difficult to land on and very dangerous to walk over, owing to the many hidden crevices and other hazards. Of course, I was the only person in the Falklands who had first-hand knowledge of conditions on Beauchêne; and, as it was known that I had made some interesting discoveries there, and was reluctant to say much until I had carried out further studies, there was a tendency to think that perhaps I was exaggerating the dangers and taking a rather dog-in-the-manger attitude.

On receiving the schedule for the forthcoming visits of the Lindblad vessel *Explorer*, I was amazed to see that a visit to Beauchêne Island was included. I was left with only one course to follow, and on 16 October wrote to the Colonial Secretary about the proposed visit, giving my reasons why I thought it should not take place. It had always been a thorn in my side that the island had been made a sanctuary rather than a reserve, and in a second letter to the Colonial Secretary I asked whether the island's status might be changed, so making Beauchêne a restricted area. This did not happen at once, but the Government fully agreed with me about the proposed visit, and in addition pointed out that the *Explorer* would be breaking the law in visiting Beauchêne before first obtaining clearance at a port of entry. Naturally I did not like having to appeal to the Government to prevent the visit to Beauchêne, but I believed that, if Lindblad Travel really were dedicated to conservation, the company would see the sense in my action.

During October I received a letter from Peter Scott informing me that General Sir Gerald Lathbury, an ornithologist of some distinction, would be passing through the Falklands early the following year. Peter asked if I could arrange for General Lathbury to see something of the bird life and learn of conservation problems in the Falklands.

Acknowledging Peter's letter, I mentioned the Agricultural Advisory Team, who were studying the colony's sheep farming industry. I had already spoken to the team and knew that they had been approached on the "goose problem". Since becoming involved with conservation in the Falklands, I had tried to keep off the question of upland geese and the efforts that farmers were making to eradicate them, for I believed that to make an issue of the matter would make things worse, and that the geese were not seriously threatened. However, it now seemed that some new and more devastating onslaught might begin, and, while remaining on the sidelines, I wanted to prepare my support in case the worst should happen. In mentioning the problem to Peter Scott, I did not ask if he would intervene, but merely if he could supply me with information on the experiments in geese grazing that had been carried out at Slimbridge. I think I did right, for the debate about goose eradication became very heated indeed.

In November, when many birds were breeding and in full song, I turned my attention to sound recording. This was an activity on which I placed a great deal of importance, having already built up a fair-sized library of recordings. I hoped that this would one day prove of scientific value, but in the meantime my work proved of financial assistance to me, as I was able to sell a lot of recordings to the BBC.

Principally to obtain some more recordings, I went to Kidney Island for a week, only two days of which proved suitable to my purpose. However, these were fine, calm days, and I was able to add two more species to the number represented in my library. The first of these was the short-eared owl, whose alarm calls I succeeded in recording. I also managed to tape the beautiful low moan that these owls make to each other at sunset, and in so doing I discovered that these calls are very regularly spaced, the interval between calls varying by little more than a second or two.

The second species that I managed to record was the grass wren, and in achieving this I had a great deal of difficulty. Though I was using a parabolic reflector and the birds were in full song, I could not approach close enough to obtain a good recording. Eventually I solved the problem by playing back part of what I had taped—a stratagem that had once worked before, with another species. No sooner had I started than a wren appeared only four or five feet away and burst into a torrent of sound. However, when I played back the bird's own song, it went quite frantic, and actually perched on the recorder!

A far less pleasant feature of my stay on Kidney Island was my discovery of large numbers of discarded beer cans and glass bottles scattered about the hut. For years Kidney had been a place that only a handful of people interested in bird life visited, but recently some people who did not know and had no interest in the island had advertised it as a place to visit, and these cans and bottles were the result. The glass bottles were especially dangerous, since they could easily start a fire, which would be devastating to a small tussac island like Kidney with its dense populations of shearwaters. Earlier I had suggested to the Government that there should be some control on visits to the island, but, when I dropped three sack-loads of crushed-up beer cans and bottles into deep water on my way back from the island, I knew that the time had come to insist that something be done. On 24 November I wrote on the matter to the Government, and said that I was prepared to act as warden myself.

In December I received a letter dated 17 November from Len Hill, who said that he was leaving for a visit to South Africa and wondered how "Grand and Steeple Jason Islands are getting on, as I have not heard anything about them. All I want is the lowest price for which they can be purchased. I am prepared to consider putting up the cash freehold." He had wanted me to telegraph him in South

Africa, but by the time I received his letter he was already on his way back to England. Mr Barton had written to him giving the price Dean Brothers were prepared to sell at, and a little later I heard from Mr Barton that an agreement had been reached. I was pleased the islands had been secured, but was sorry not to have been kept informed on the details of the final agreement, and that the purchase was not to be a joint effort with the WWF.

During November and December I made two trips to Volunteer Point to obtain final figures for the number of young king penguins on the rookery. Anybody visiting the rookery at this period of the year and not familiar with the birds' breeding cycle would probably have been puzzled by the scene. There were birds in courtship display, birds incubating, adults and young moulting, and young covered in fluffy brown down.

King penguins take a year to reach maturity, so, as the adults have to feed their young for eleven or twelve months, the complete breeding cycle takes over a year. A pair starting to breed in November will therefore, not start breeding again until about January (i.e. midsummer) of the season following; and in the next season the same pair may not be ready to breed until March (i.e. autumn). As this is late for birds to be laying, the pair generally forgo breeding until spring of the next season; or if they attempt, it is probable that they will lose the egg. The result is that the birds generally breed two seasons in three, and that in the summer months there is considerable variety in the birds' activities and in the maturity of their young.

In December I took General Lathbury to Volunteer Point and we counted fifty-four king penguins on the rookery. The beach itself was covered with lines of Magellans coming ashore, and Sir Gerald remarked that it looked just like the beach at Dunkirk, with lines of soldiers waiting to be taken off! General Lathbury obviously was impressed by what he saw in the Falklands and, just as I had been, was surprised at the vast amount of bird life there and the little known about it outside the islands themselves.

Once I had become free of the fur farm, my idea of Christmas was to get away, even from celebrations. Annie and I spoke about this, and Shona and Sharron were quite thrilled with our suggestion that we spend Christmas on Kidney Island. We could still take the usual goodies, but could please ourselves about when and how we tackled

Magellan Penguin

Magellan penguin (*Spheniscus magellanicus*) feeding under water on forms of 'krill'. The species is commonly found in many areas of the Falklands but prefers the more accessible coasts on which to form its nesting burrow. Locally called 'Jackass' penguins, they are not to be confused with the South African Jackass penguin which is a different species. The name 'Jackass' probably derives from their braying calls.

them. Christmas in the southern hemisphere is of course, at mid-summer; and even the girls, who were born in the Falklands but had spent some years in England, found the lack of cold weather odd.

It certainly turned out an unconventional Christmas! We were out recording sooty shearwaters until 4 a.m. on Christmas morning, and our Christmas lunch consisted of ham sandwiches and Christmas cake! But what a fantastic day it was. With the sun beating down on the island, the heat in the tussac grass was terrific; and for company we had hundreds of rockhopper penguins. This was the first of three Christmases we spent on the island—all of them memorable; and I am sure that all of us, but particularly Shona and Sharron, will remember them as among the most enjoyable experienced.

On Christmas night we were again recording sooty shearwaters. I was always careful not to force the girls' interest in these things, and made it a rule that, when I went out recording late at night, I took the girls only if they volunteered to join me. I believe that this encouraged them to develop a genuine interest in wildlife, and Shona is already quite positive that she wants to work in this field.

Not all the shearwaters on Kidney Island were sooty shearwaters. On earlier occasions I had sighted a black and white variety, the greater shearwater. This species normally breeds on Tristan da Cunha, and visits the Falklands only in the course of migration; but some years earlier Woods had found a solitary pair breeding on Kidney, and I had noted a number of these birds in the rafts that shearwaters formed on the water before starting their evening flight into the island. This Christmas evening I decided to keep a close watch for any greater shearwaters, and to attempt to locate them as they landed in the tussac. I noted that the incoming birds kept to a definite flight pattern, which made it fairly easy to know where the best place to watch from would be.

Hardly had we begun our vigil when a greater shearwater passed over and suddenly dropped into the grass only a few feet away. A search revealed nothing: the bird had vanished into the thick tussac and gone down one of the hundreds of burrows thereabouts. However, I noted that the bird's call was very different from that of the sooty shearwaters, and, with the help of earphones and the parabolic reflector, was able to pick out where the calls appeared to be coming from. In this way we discovered two pairs of breeding greater shearwaters that night and later found a few more. From an ornithological standpoint, this discovery was important, and it greatly enhanced the value of Kidney as a reserve.

In January 1970 I wrote to Dr Vollmar explaining that Len Hill was prepared to purchase Steeple and Grand Jason. I said that I was sorry that the WWF would not be involved in the purchase, but expressed my belief that the islands would be in good hands. In addition, I told Dr Vollmar that I had offered to act as warden for the islands and hoped to undertake a programme of reseeding natural grasses. Len was pleased with my offer to act as warden and asked if I would keep an eye on the islands for him.

Early in January 1970 I was again preparing for a visit by Lind-blad Travel, which for one reason and another, had not operated any visits to the Falklands in 1969. The *Explorer* was planned to call at the islands in January and late February, bringing many people keenly interested in wildlife. The prospects for a successful demon-stration of the benefit that these trips could bring to the islands were good.

I kept conservationists well informed about the progress of plans for wildlife tourism, and was concerned to show that my interest in the idea was not guided by the profit motive. In fact, I was later accused of this, by some people with very short memories; but my real attitude may be judged from a letter I wrote to Dr Vollmar on the subject:

> Tourism is now becoming much more of a reality here in the Islands, and as I have stated for some years now, could be a strong lever for future conservation here. The well-publicised Antarctic tourist vessel will again be visiting the islands presently, and we have made arrangements for it to visit certain carefully controlled wildlife areas. It is hoped that this new industry will mature, although I hope at a slow rate which will enable us to keep more control over visits to wildlife regions. Fortunately at present I have been fully responsible locally for these visits, and therefore have been in the position to direct these to suitable areas. How-ever, as might be expected, interest is suddenly going to be taken by other parties who wish only to reap benefit on a short term policy. In an effort to reduce this threat, proposals have been put forward to bring in legislation for the control of visitors to some of our more accessible wild life areas. My main concern is for such areas as Kidney Island Reserve, which lies within reach of Stanley.

In his reply Dr Vollmar said that he was very interested to hear how things were going, and that he was with me entirely in hoping that developments could be kept under control. He also indicated (and I later had confirmation) that Len Hill proposed leaving Steeple and Grand Jason to the WWF in his will.

The *Explorer* was expected on 11 January, and to save time was to be cleared at Fox Bay, on West Falkland. I, as guide, was to fly out to Fox Bay and stay with the ship until she reached Stanley three days later and was cleared to leave the islands. It was years since a vessel had been cleared at Fox Bay, and, though it created no great problems, a lot of details had to be arranged. These and numerous other matters concerning the ship's visit to the Falklands kept me fully occupied for some while.

On the 4th the Governor rang me to say that he had received news that the ship had caught fire and that the trip might be off! In addition, I had still not had confirmation of the ship's exact date of arrival, so on the 6th I sent a telegram to New York requesting information. The next day the Governor contacted the Foreign Office for news. The whole business was becoming embarrassing, for, as the person who was arranging the ship's cruise about the islands, I knew the least! To make matters worse, the Falkland Islands Company, which had unsuccessfully tried to obtain the agency for Lindblad's voyages to the Falklands, was keeping an eagle eye on proceedings. The company had been annoyed when I arranged the *Navarino*'s visit in 1968, and was no more pleased about the *Explorer*'s proposed visit. The company's manager and I had already exchanged strong words on the subject, and I saw that the matter was not closed yet.

On 13 January I eventually received word that the ship had caught fire and was in Buenos Aires being repaired. This news brought yet another fall of remarks about the hopelessness of expecting tourism to be a success in the Falklands; but, although the first voyage had to be cancelled, the ship did in fact make two trips to the islands that summer. These were a success and convinced me that tourism and wildlife conservation could indeed work to each other's benefit if properly organised.

Lars Lindblad visited the Falklands on both voyages and was obviously amazed at what he saw. I had some long discussions with him about forthcoming trips and about my aims with regard to tourism and conservation. We did not agree on all points, but basically it seemed that we could work together.

One of the points he raised was the possibility of making visits to Kidney Island. I explained to him that Kidney was far too small to have some eighty or ninety people trooping over it, and he accepted my judgement on the matter. However, I saw that, if other tourist boats came to Stanley I would be unlikely to have much say in where they might or might not go. Again I wrote to the Government putting forward suggestions for the more effective control of Kidney Island, and I laid special stress on the need to limit the number who could visit it at any one time.

To my great disappointment, I obtained no response at all. Either the Government simply was not interested, or the matter was seen as too insignificant to warrant attention. Still, I had registered my concern, and, if nothing else, I had made the Government wildlife file a bit fatter!

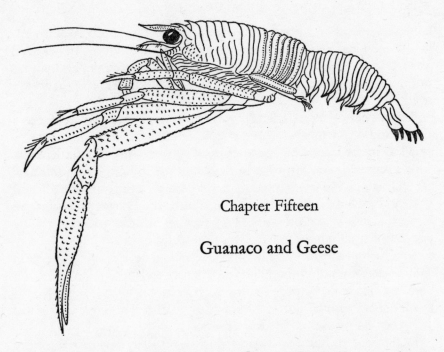

Chapter Fifteen

Guanaco and Geese

In the early 1930s a number of South American species were introduced into the Falklands. Among these were the rhea (a relative of
the ostrich), skunks, foxes, parrots, otters and guanaco. The skunks
and birds soon perished, but the otters, a marine type from Patagonia, were more fortunate, and a few may remain in some isolated
creeks. Foxes were placed on several islands in the West Falklands
and continue to thrive. The guanaco were placed on Staats Island,
an island about four miles long and lying a few miles from Weddell
—again, in the west. These llama-type animals thrived until there
were some two or three hundred on the island. In 1956 over a
hundred were shot, and three years later a further 286 were killed, as
it was considered that the animals were eating themselves out of
existence. How many remained after this I do not know, but they
were more or less left in peace again until about 1969.

I had several times thought of visiting Staats to learn more of
these animals, but while they were being left alone there seemed no
reason for urgency. However in 1969 I heard that it was planned to
kill off the guanaco and repopulate the island with sheep, and that a
boat party from New Island had cornered a herd of forty-eight and
massacred them with automatic rifles.

Though I knew little of guanaco, and realised that they were not
indigenous to the Falklands, I thought that they should be given

some chance to survive in the islands, and that the decision to exterminate them had been taken with very little thought. It was well known that the skins of the young were quite valuable, and yet no one had considered whether they could be farmed alongside the sheep.

The owner of Staats Island lived in the Argentine and, so far as I could find out, had never seen the island. The running of his farms was left in the hands of managers and an overseer, Charlie Robertson, a retired sheep farmer who had worked in both Patagonia and the Falklands. He was a huge man, dedicated to the outdoor life and with an immense knowledge of sheep farming. However, he had no great interest in wildlife, and I knew that on the question of the guanaco I should have to tread very carefully.

Not being certain whether I could persuade Charlie Robertson against exterminating the guanaco, I wrote to Roddy Napier asking whether he would be prepared to keep a few on West Point. He was quite enthusiastic about the idea of a small study herd, and so in July 1969 I approached Mr Robertson.

I explained to him that I had heard about the plans to kill off the herds, and asked whether he would have any objection to my going to Staats to see the herd first and to catch a pair with which to start a study herd on West Point. Naturally, he thought that I was mad, but said that it was up to me if I wanted to go chasing after guanaco. He thought them pests and wanted them shot, but he had no idea when his Weddell Island manager, Bob Ferguson, would be doing the job. It was clear from this meeting that I certainly would not get anywhere with suggestions for finding out whether the guanaco could coexist with sheep or be farmed for their skins.

It was now midwinter, and, as most farms have some free time at this season, I was worried that the guanaco would be shot before I could visit Staats. Accordingly I wrote to Bob Ferguson explaining about my visit and saying that ideally I should like to make it in December, when the females would be in calf or having their young. Bob replied that he had thought of going to Staats in October, but was quite prepared to wait. His letter gave me the feeling that he was rather sorry that the guanaco had to go.

In the course of writing to the WWF about the Jason Islands, I mentioned the question of the guanaco and, without attacking the decision to kill them off, said that I hoped to move some animals and establish a study herd. Dr Vollmar asked me to keep in touch on the matter and said that he would inform Peter Scott, Chairman of the Survival Service of the IUCN. I had already written to Peter asking for information about the status of the guanaco in South America, and he said that he would see what could be found. At this stage all I wanted to do was to obtain facts about the animals, so that when I went to Staats I would know something of the animals I was handling.

When the summer came I was continually on the lookout for a chance to go to Staats, but bad weather, changes of plan by *Explorer*, and the difficulty of finding anyone to accompany me prevented my going, and by March I was worried that soon it would be too late. In addition, there were the problems of catching and transporting the guanaco. Catching them would be made easier by using a "drug gun", but *Gleam* was hardly big enough to take the animals to West Point and that meant that I should have to obtain the services of a larger vessel. Only the merchant vessel *Forrest*, which was due to leave Stanley for Weddell and West Point at about the middle of March could fit this into her itinerary, and it would be necessary to have captured the animals and have them ready for moving by the time *Forrest* reached Staats. This meant enlisting the help of the Beaver and fitting into the plane three passengers (this was the minimum number I thought would be needed for the job) and all the equipment needed. Fortunately the Air Service were willing to help, and, though the Beaver had not landed at Staats before, expected that landing would present no problems. Two friends, Don Davidson and David Hardy, agreed to join me, and on 18 March we packed into the Beaver and made the 140-mile journey from Stanley to Staats.

There are over 230 islands in the Falklands, each with its own quite distinctive character. Staats, an island about four miles long and half a mile wide, with very prominent hills dotting its length, is no exception. Its coastline is a mixture of low-lying sandy beaches and sheer cliffs, the highest of which lie at the southern end of the island. There, rising 400 feet above sea level and severed from the main island by a wide chasm, is perhaps the most impressive stack in the Falklands.

It was striking how well the guanaco matched their surroundings. So strongly did I feel this that I really began to believe that Staats would die as an island without those creatures, and that those who wished to kill them off would change their minds if only they would come and watch them as I was doing.

The guanaco were divided into small herds, each of which had its own territory and lookout point—usually the top of one of the hills. There the oldest male of the herd would be stationed as sentinel, continually alert for danger. We could not even move out of the small hut on the island without being spotted by one of these sentinels, which would immediately start neighing. On hearing this, the herd would stop grazing, watch for a few moments and then bound away to safety.

I noticed that, in moving about the island, the guanaco usually kept to well-defined tracks, some of which passed round rocky ridges where I thought it might be possible to lie in wait for them. However, though I spent hours wedged between rocks or otherwise concealed close to these routes, drug-gun at the ready, I had no success. Generally something would disturb the animals before they came within range; and, on the one occasion when a herd did pass me by, I was so placed that I did not see them until they were right alongside, and they hurtled by at about thirty-five miles per hour. I fired at point-blank range into the group and watched spellbound as the dart spiralled past necks, bodies and legs, and buried itself harmlessly in the ground. By the time that I had reloaded, the animals were round the next hillside, still travelling at speed.

Later I came across a lone animal feeding. Fortunately she was on lower ground, and, by making use of some fairly long grass, I was able to crawl to within fifteen yards of her. My first shot missed, but, as the gun was gas-fired and silent, I was able to reload, and this time was successful. However, on closer inspection I found that I had brought down an old female who had probably been thrown out of her herd as past calf-bearing. At length I decided to let her go.

One day Don surprised a small group of guanaco and was able to run down a calf that was with them. This animal turned out to be a male in very good condition, the only problem being that it was still suckling and would require hand-feeding. We had not expected to find young animals so late in the season, and had nothing to use as a feeding bottle; so, using a method that I had learned years before for getting calves to drink from a bucket, I sat for hours with the young guanaco, dipping my finger in diluted condensed milk and getting him to suck it. Eventually he became used to sipping direct from a billycan, but we were very short of milk and did not have enough to last until *Forrest* came to collect us. I radioed West Point to ask Roddy if he could arrange for the Beaver to drop us some milk, and the next day we heard that the aircraft was due in the area. Ian Campbell, the pilot, had apparently inquired about the size of the animal—which could only mean that he was thinking of flying it direct to West Point!

Before the Beaver arrived, I gave the guanaco an injection of tranquilliser and bandaged his long spindly legs with mutton cloth, in order to protect them. When Ian saw the cargo—virtually a bundle of legs!—he said that its size was no problem, and so our valuable capture was loaded onto the aircraft. Just over half an hour later the guanaco was safely landed at West Point, apparently none the worse for his flight. A couple of days later we were picked up by *Forrest*, but we had not succeeded in capturing another animal.

Fed on cow's milk, the young guanaco grew at an amazing rate and became very tame, in fact too tame. I became worried that, if we managed to obtain a mate for him, he might not breed. Being so docile, he developed a habit of running to and jumping up at people. If one has seen these creatures fighting in the wild, one soon realises that such habits have to be watched very carefully. I asked Roddy and Lilly if they could try to get the guanaco away from the settlement and so make him more independent, but this proved impossible. Unfortunately, the animal's tameness proved his downfall and so paid a heavy blow to my hopes of establishing a study herd outside Staats.

With winter approaching, field trips became less and less practicable and I was spending most of my time writing and painting. If I were to be able to stay in the islands, it was essential for me to sell a certain number of articles, photographs and paintings every year. Annie had her wage, but this could not support all of us and I felt very strongly about the need to be self-supporting: if I could not manage to make a living out of my work in conservation and related activities, how could I convince others of the potential economic value of the islands' wildlife? Of course, merely the fact that I had no regular nine-to-five job suggested to many that I was living off Ann's wage or had some mysterious private income. Very few were aware of my writing and painting activities, or of the fact that I would often paint seven days a week and for ten or twelve hours a day.

That winter proved an important turning point for my painting activities. Hal Seielstad, whom I had met on board the *Navarino* and who had shown a great deal of interest in my painting, was sure there was a good market for the type of work I was doing, and asked

me to assemble a collection of ten or twelve paintings and send them
to him in San Francisco, where he would investigate the market. On
11 April nine of my paintings went on exhibition at the Maxwell
Gallery in San Francisco—as Hal wrote, "the West's most prestigi-
ous gallery". The gallery sold them at $125 each, of which I re-
ceived half; but, though this was still a low return in terms of the
number of hours' work I had put into each picture, this was twice
as much as I had been getting from private sales. Naturally I was
delighted.

As the paintings sold quickly, the Maxwell Gallery wanted ten
paintings available all the time, and Hal was for ever asking me to
turn out more pictures. This I could not do, for, although I worked
long hours at painting, I could not operate as a production line or
devote all my time to painting, from which I sometimes needed a
rest. I said that the most I could turn out in a single year was twenty-
five pictures. I could have produced more if I had paid less attention
to detail, but it was not in my nature to do so.

That same winter we again had housing problems to face, as our
landlord had sold the house that we were renting and the new owner
wanted to move in. Annie approached the Government again to see
whether she would qualify for married quarters, and to our great
relief we learned that she could have a house. This turned out to be
a large bungalow to the west of the town, and had large windows
giving me all the light I wanted for painting. For the first time in
years we unpacked many treasures that, owing to lack of space, had
been stored away. Having space to move about in gave us all a
boost, and I was able to get a great deal more done.

On 14 May I wrote to Dr Vollmar to tell him the result of the
guanaco expedition, and at about the same time I heard that, despite
numerous delays in carrying it out, the decision to kill off the herds
still stood. I wondered if a word from the WWF or IUCN might
perhaps persuade Mr Robertson to keep the herds, so I asked Dr
Vollmar if he could arrange for someone to write.

As Chairman of the IUCN Survival Service Commission, Peter
Scott wrote to Mr Robertson about the interest in the guanaco and
in the possibility of establishing a herd on West Point, and pointed
out that the guanaco might become a valuable tourist attraction. He
went on to say that the Commission would be enormously grateful
for any help in ensuring the guanaco's survival in the Falklands.

Mr Robertson, however, was none too pleased at being told "what he had to do with his guanaco", and the local radio station did not help by broadcasting a news item in which it was stated that we had been catching guanaco on Staats and moving them to West Point specifically with the idea of establishing a tourist attraction. Certainly the animals would be an *added* attraction to visitors, but that was hardly the main reason for our interest in them.

Dr Vollmar also wrote to Mr Robertson, and, as I was convinced that we would have problems, I wrote to Bob Ferguson on Weddell Island asking if he could leave the guanaco as late as possible. I made a point of seeing Charlie Robertson and discussing the whole situation with him, but got little further. He was clearly annoyed at the letter from Peter, even though it had been phrased as a request and not a demand. Simply to obtain a mate for the animal that had been captured would be something, and I still hoped that a small herd might be retained on Staats, to run with the sheep. However, it seemed to be generally believed that sheep could not live with guanaco, because of competition for grazing; that guanaco poisoned water supplies; and that guanaco carried scab and sheep ticks. There was, of course, no proof for these excuses, as there was so far not a single sheep on Staats.

On my first visit to Staats I had observed that the guanaco fed mainly on coarse vegetation rather than on the finer grasses preferred by sheep. The animals nearly always kept to higher ground, where there was a lot of diddle-dee and spiky fescue, which sheep would not eat. As I wanted to learn more about the guanaco's feeding habits, I began planning another visit to Staats.

In August the Sheep Owners Association held its main meeting in Stanley. This and similar gatherings gave me an excellent chance to meet and talk with farmers from all over the Falklands, picking up much useful information in the process. We all knew each other and were on reasonable friendly terms, but I knew that most of them looked upon me as "that crazy bird man" and that it had been said that the Falklands would be a better place without the geese and the conservationists! Geese, which were generally classified as vermin, were almost invariably mentioned at the Association's meetings; and, though I was not a sheep farmer and therefore was unable to attend, I knew from the reports I received that little effort was made to discuss whether geese really were vermin, and that the meeting would generally confine itself to voting for bigger reductions in the number of these birds.

At the August 1970 meeting of the Association, the question of the upland goose was raised yet again. The Agricultural Advisory Team had been working in the islands for some time, and though no one in the team was qualified to study the upland goose, it was understood that the team were looking into the "problem" and would cover it in their report. Mr Sydney Miller, an ardent advocate of goose eradication, remarked that one of the team had stated that the geese had to go, and following this a vote was taken on the question, with a majority in favour of destroying the geese. Furthermore, mention was made of controlling the geese by means of a poison or stupefying drugs. When I heard of this I was horrified, and decided that the time had come to break my rule to leave the goose issue alone. I had no idea what poison or drugs might be used, or how they would be used, but I suspected that they would be spread on the grasslands on which the geese fed. If this were so, what would be the effect on the sheep?

On 15 August I wrote on the matter to Peter Scott and Dr Vollmar, explaining that the use of a drug or poison had been mentioned. I made it clear, however, that nothing had yet been decided officially and that it would be unwise to act as if it had. For the time being I thought that the main need was for investigations of the geese, to see for what they could and could not be blamed.

When the Agricultural Team's report was published, I was surprised to find that, although it put forward the opinion that the upland goose was a nuisance to the sheep farming industry, no mention was made of using poison or drugs to control populations. Later I began to suspect that the report had been "tamed down", but in the meantime I found myself blamed for stirring up the goose issue. Peter Scott had written to the Colonial Secretary, Mr J. A. Jones, mentioning that he understood that the Agricultural Team had advocated the reduction of goose populations in the Falklands, and that mention had been made of using poisonous bait. However, the letter's main emphasis was on the suggestion that a careful study of the geese should be carried out first. The Colonial Secretary, in his reply to Peter Scott, stated that, so far as he was aware, no specific suggestion to use poisonous bait had been made, and that, if any such proposal did come before the Legislature, "it would receive most careful evaluation". However, as I pointed out to Mr Jones, the Legislature was composed largely of farmers. and such "careful evaluation" would almost certainly go against the geese. My concern was to take a balanced view; but my position was rendered very difficult by the fact that others had been sending to various conservation bodies in England exaggerated reports claiming that the geese were about to be completely annihilated! I was now suspected of these remarks, and thus my attempts at ensuring some moderation were greatly hampered.

For some months the question of the geese swayed gently backwards and forwards. In March 1971 the Ministry of Overseas Development sent Messrs Thorne and MacKenzie to the Falklands to consider the Agricultural Team's findings and the reactions of farmers to what had been said about the geese. I felt that it was desirable to voice my opinions on this issue, and on 19 March wrote to Thorne and MacKenzie explaining my views and my interest in conservation. I said,

> The regrettable fact is that as yet nothing, or very little, is known about the geese in the islands. We don't even know what the true population is. Proposals have been made for such studies to be carried out, and I am currently investigating the possibilities of obtaining finances to carry out the ground work. I personally view the geese in the islands as a proved asset, in that they supply a valuable protein. At the same time, I would be the first to agree that they can in certain cases cause damage. This I believe is true where crops have been sown. There may also be, in certain cases, competition with sheep for grass. However, these things have to be proved or disproved by careful study.

I continue by explaining my feelings about wasteful destruction, and suggested that, if the geese had to be reduced, some industry should utilise the cropping.

Having heard Thorne and MacKenzie in a local broadcast, I gathered they were not pro-geese. I think this is borne out by the fact that I never received even an acknowledgement of my letter!

As a next step, I approached the Government to see whether I could obtain support for a survey of the geese. The answer was firm and negative, but, judging from the way the results of my seal survey had been received, perhaps this was just as well.

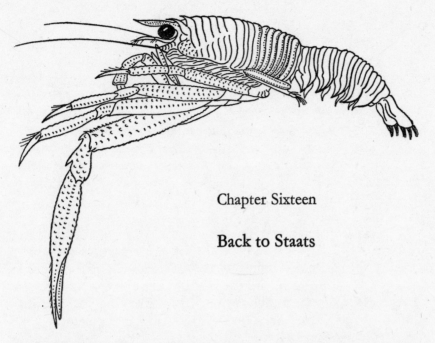

Chapter Sixteen

Back to Staats

During August 1970 I met Bob Ferguson in Stanley and thus had an excellent chance to talk to him about the guanaco situation. Don Davidson and I explained to him what we had discovered about the animals and the island, and said that we thought there was a good case for keeping a small herd on Staats, even if sheep were placed there. Bob, whom we were to discover had never been over Staats, though he had landed there, appeared to be interested in what we told him. The outcome was that he gave permission for a second visit to the island, so that the feeding habits of the guanaco could be studied further.

On 7 September I flew out to Staats with Annie and our friend Sue Wright. Sue's husband, Peter, was a young doctor working for a while in the Falklands. Both were keen outdoor types, and it had originally been planned that Peter would go with us as well, but work had prevented this.

As we flew out, the sky was bright and cloudless, and the sea like a mirror. Approaching Staats, we could see the entire Weddell Island group and as far north as West Point. Jim made a complete circuit of the island before landing, so that I could film the cliffs on the west side and so that Sue and Annie could see what to expect.

Taking such equipment as a cine camera and sound recorder meant that we had had to work out very carefully what our daily food requirements would be, and then, going on the total weight allowed for the flight, work out how many days we could spend on Staats. Our allowance gave us seven days' food with nothing to spare; so when I booked the flight I made it clear that we would have to return in a week. While unloading the Beaver, we again discussed this with Jim, as our small radio transmitter had a rather limited range and it was best ot organise such matters before we were left.

During our stay on Staats, we discovered that there was no doubt that the herds were feeding on the coarser vegetation such as diddle-dee. Even after winter the grasslands were untouched, and, although we saw one herd feeding in the tussac, it was clear that they did this only while sheltering.

The weather proved very changeable, with calm, warm conditions on some days and snow on others! One particular day will always remain in my memory. Being windless, it was ideal for recording, and I had gone out to record the calls of guanaco. On this occasion I purposely walked up the centre of the valleys, so that the male sentinels posted on the surrounding peaks would not fail to see me. The results were excellent, for not only the sentinels, but also other animals in the herd, started to call, the sound echoing back and forth across the valleys. As one herd stopped, so another started. To add atmosphere, several pipits burst into song above me, and the soft, distant murmur of surf could be heard. For me, this was one of those special moments when all the frustrations of my work were blotted out and I felt at complete harmony with nature.

Soon after, the weather turned very cold, and, as the only form of heating in the hut was the primus stove, which we could only use for cooking, we spent much of the daylight hours walking about to keep warm. This sharpened our appetites and so reduced our food supply, which by Saturday was so low that all we had left for Sunday was soup and tea. I was not too bothered, as we were due to be picked up on Monday, but, when, on Saturday night, we listened in on our radio to the flight schedules for Monday, we found that we were not listed! On Sunday I tried to send out a message on the transmitter, but could make no contact; and the same happened on Monday. Much later we found out that Roddy, who had loaned us the set, had forgotten to change the batteries!

When we realised that we would not be collected on Monday, we started to look around for food, and took a hint from the island's foxes. These had been brought to the island at the same time as the guanaco, and appeared to do well from feeding off the beaches.

(*above*) An adult pair of Rockhopper penguins with their chick in a rookery on Kidney Island.
(*below*) A Gentoo penguin feeding its chick.

(*above*) Black-browed albatross coming in to feed their young on Bird Island.

The endangered Johnny Rooks on Beauchêne Island. They nested within a few feet of the Rockhopper Penguins on which they preyed.

The author looking out over the huge colony of albatross and penguin on Jason Island. It stretches (top left) out as far as the eye can see.

A Black-browed albatross on its nest with a penguin near by.

Often we came across small areas littered with the shells of limpets that foxes had brought from the coast and fed upon. How they prised them from the rocks I do not know, but having seen them exhibit their skills at overturning rocks and quickly grabbing the small fish that sheltered underneath, I had no doubt that they had found a solution to the problem.

On the beaches we found a plentiful supply of mussels, but the amount of meat provided by one mussel was so small that it required vast quantities to make a reasonable meal. Another excellent source of food was tussac grass, the base of the stems holding tender shoots that taste like horse chestnuts; but, again, there was the problem of collecting enough. Our remaining provisions were half a tin of milk, some tea, and two or three packets of soup, so from Sunday on our meals consisted of a stew of tussac shoots and mussels cooked in soup. It was good but not very filling, so we felt hungry all the time.

In the hope of adding some fish to our diet, and having left my fishing gear in Stanley, I tried to make a fish hook from a safety pin. However, though I got the shape right, I was unable to temper the metal to stop it bending. Since fishing was out, we tried cooking seaweed, but it turned out so tough and unpalatable that we decided to keep to mussel and tussac stew!

By Tuesday we were feeling very empty, and still there was no mention of us in the flight schedules. Our only hope was that Peter or someone else would realise that we were not overstaying intentionally and raise the matter with the Air Service.

As Tuesday evening was calm, I decided, despite being cold and hungry, to try recording the calls of the foxes. Surrounding the hut and stretching the full length of the sand beach was a thick belt of tussac. Foxes had been calling from this area, and I settled down to wait at a spot where they had been tracking back and forth. How long I waited I cannot remember, but I was uncomfortable and very cold. As darkness fell, cloud came up from the south, and the moon, hidden behind Tea Island, presented that island in silhouette. The scene, with dark clouds slowly moving across the moonlit sky, was beautiful but eerie.

Quite soon a full moon appeared over the shoulder of Tea Island, and at the same instant a fox began to call—barking, yelping and screaming. As soon as this animal stopped, another began; and then, in answer, another, some distance off. To get these distant calls I turned up the recording level, but no sooner had I done this than an ear-piercing yelp came through the earphones from a fox hidden only a few feet away in the tussac. Slowly her yelping—for I had decided that this was a vixen—changed to a scream; and, as her call changed, so the hair on my head bristled. I soon forgot my hunger, and discomfort, and became totally caught up in recording this extraordinary performance. I treasure that tape, not only because of the calls of the foxes, but also because it brings back that moment very vividly indeed. Annie and Sue had sat up in the hut listening, and we all agreed that the foxes had been making a great deal more noise that evening than on previous nights, when the moon had not appeared. We concluded that they were calling to the moon. The following night I again went out before the moon came up; and, the moment it appeared, the foxes started to call.

We were on Staats for another two days before the Beaver came to take us off, and then it came only because Shona—my eight-year-old daughter—insisted that we had food for only a week, and had got Roddy to make a booking for us! Luckily it was a beautiful day when we left, and this slightly eased the torment to our stomachs. As we loaded the Beaver I purposely stood an empty milk tin on a rock where Jim could see it, and as we moved off made some remark about squeezing the tin dry. He made no comment—just added insult to injury by taking out a flask of coffee and a box of sandwiches once we were airborne, and tucking in!

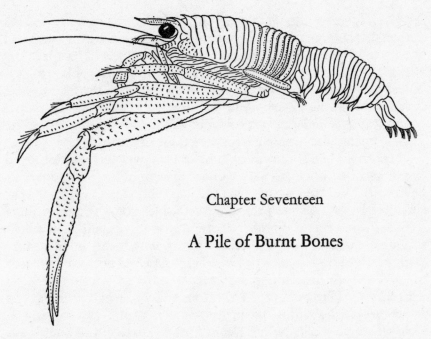

Chapter Seventeen

A Pile of Burnt Bones

In July I heard from Len Hill that in October or November he would be coming down to the Falklands to look at his "kingdom", the newly acquired Steeple and Grand Jason islands, and that he wished to collect some penguins while he was there. He briefly mentioned that he would try to charter a seaplane in Montevideo, Uruguay (over a thousand miles away), and with this fly down to Stanley and out to the Jasons. Len finished his letter by saying that he would like the landing filmed and that he would bring a plaque to commemorate the occasion and secure to a prominent rock somewhere on one of his islands. It immediately occurred to me that there would be no need for a plaque: a wrecked seaplane would be prominent enough! Len had not yet set eyes on those remote islands, and knew little of the treacherous seas surrounding them.

Eventually I managed to dissuade him from using an aircraft and he began to think of chartering a boat instead. His plans for this fell through, and I heard that he would be coming on the *Darwin* from Montevideo on 21 October. Pending his arrival, he asked if I could do my best to arrange for a boat to the Jasons.

The only boat available that could both make the trip and carry crates of penguins was the *Forrest*. She made scheduled voyages around the islands and could perhaps arrange a diversion to Steeple or Grand Jason, but, as she travelled west only once in four to six weeks and Len would be coming only for a fortnight, there was no chance that she could both take him and bring him back. Even if the vessel could spare a day from her schedule, this would hardly allow enough time for collecting penguins and filming. I spoke to Jack Sollis about *Forrest*'s schedule, and found that the only time during Len's stay that the vessel would be near the Jasons was when Len had to leave the Falklands. This would be ideal for taking us off the Jasons, but left the problem of getting there in the first place.

I now thought of the Beaver. It had flown over the Jasons several times, and had once landed at Grand Jason. Why not again? To begin with, Jim Kerr was against the idea, but, when I explained the situation, he said he was prepared to consider going provided there were someone with a working transmitter on the island, and a boat waiting to receive the Beaver. As Jim pointed out, if he had an engine failure on the water off the Jasons, he did not want to fetch up on the South American coast weeks later!

Clearly, I had to get out to the Jasons ready to receive the Beaver. *Forrest* would be within about thirty miles of the Jasons early in October, three weeks before Len was due to arrive, and could take me out to Steeple Jason with the necessary supplies and all the equipment needed for receiving the Beaver and collecting penguins. The prospect of spending three weeks alone on Steeple Jason appealed to me enormously, and, though it was annoying considered as a preparation for one landing on the Beaver, I decided that this was what I would do.

Before leaving on this trip I wanted to visit Volunteer Lagoon to check on the number of king penguin chicks that had survived the winter and to make an attempt at observing and filming the birth of an elephant seal pup. I flew out on 3 October, Ian putting the Beaver down on the lagoon.

In March, at the end of the king penguins' breeding season, I had counted twenty-four young and eggs. I hoped that the survival rate would be high, but to my great disappointment, I found seven dead and only fourteen survivors on the rookery. Some of the dead young had obviously starved to death, and I was at a loss to know why their parents should have deserted them. Certainly the remaining chicks, which looked quite ridiculous waddling about in their deep brown coats of down, were being fed. Suddenly there flashed into my memory a story I had been told of a cine film that had been taken on that very spot and that had shown people attempting to make the penguins leave their eggs and move about in display. I wished that those same people could see what I then saw. Perhaps it would impress on them how vulnerable these birds were, and how important it was that they should not be disturbed.

The earliest records I had of elephant seal being born were for mid September, so I had estimated that pupping would be at its height in early October. Unfortunately I miscalculated by three or four days, for on walking the coast between Volunteer and Cow Bay, I saw that three-quarters of the cows had pupped a short while before. I never did see a birth, though I sat for many hours watching a cow that I thought was having contractions. As it was getting very cold and it seemed that birth was not imminent after all, I went for a walk, and on returning an hour later found the cow nursing a new-born pup. There are plenty such disappointments in working with wildlife, but there is always some unexpected compensation.

Later the same day the wind dropped, offering me a good opportunity to record the odd high-pitched call that I had heard the young king penguins making as they were being fed. It was late by the time I had succeeded, and in the process I had also recorded the trumpeting calls of the adults. When I started to play these back, three young immediately came over to me uttering their high-pitched calls, which showed that the adults' trumpeting meant that food was available. As I slowly walked away from the colony, the youngsters chased after me, just as I had seen them chase after their parents earlier in the day.

The following day I returned to the place where I just missed seeing an elephant seal being born, and was horrified to find several dead pups lying along the beach. One, which appeared to have died only a short while before, was lying in the surf with blood oozing from its neck. Puzzled as to what had happened, I decided to save the skin and attempt to discover how the pup had been killed. Later I concluded that the cows themselves had been responsible, having accidentally killed the pups as they tried to whisk them away from the harem bull, who was defending his territory against a rival.

As I had two miles to go to reach camp, and the skin was wet and heavy, I tied a piece of cord to it and dragged it over the ground. About two hours later, I was amazed to see four turkey vultures following the exact course I had taken with the skin. I had been very painstaking in the skinning and had not left any fat or meat upon it; also I had washed the skin in sea water. Since there could be nothing left on the ground for the birds to see, it appeared that they were following the track by scent. Clearly, in locating carrion, vultures cannot rely entirely on sight.

A few days later I returned to Stanley, packed up stores for a month's stay on Steeple Jason, and prepared for *Forrest*'s departure. By 13 October we had reached Pebble Island, the owners of which had until recently been owners of Steeple and Grand Jason. They had sold the islands because of the difficulties of working them; but, in speaking to two of the men who had worked on the islands, I found a keen interest in how things were there, and even a little envy that I was on my way back!

After passing up Byron Sound, we reached Carcass Island, where I spoke to Kitty and Cecil about the schedules for radio contact while I was on Steeple Jason. The next port of call was Sedge Island, and Jack Sollis said that, if we cleared the island that morning, he would make straight for Steeple, about thirty miles away. Things went as planned, and at 2 p.m.—almost at dead low water, when the swell is at its minimum—we reached Steeple.

At about fifty yards out, the swell was running at two or three feet, which would have made landing difficult; but, in the gulch where we landed the gear, the water was calm. I never did discover the reason for this odd behaviour of the tides off the coast of Steeple, but thought that perhaps there was a current running parallel with the shore and having a buffering effect on the swell.

I found that the island had visibly changed since the sheep had gone. The hills, of course, were the same; but the grass, which before had been closely cropped, was now almost knee-high. In addition, there was a marked decrease in the number of upland geese. There was no reason to think that anyone had disturbed them, so I wondered if there had been an increase in the number of Johnny Rooks, which preyed on geese. Another thought I had was that perhaps the geese found the grass too long now there were no sheep to crop it. It was ironic, but perhaps the best way to get rid of geese was to move out the sheep that feed on the same grasslands!

One of the most impressive changes in the island's vegetation was the spread of tussac. On the north-facing slopes, the sheep had completely eaten it out; but now, especially in the area used by Gentoo penguins, it had begun to re-establish itself, making use of the soil enriched by the penguins. There were about 9,000 Gentoos on the main rookery, all busy nest-building. Little notice was taken as I walked round the outskirts of the colony, which was much quieter than colonies that are frequently visited by egg collectors and so on. It was difficult to conceive that the penguin colonies on Steeple had suffered worse depredation than almost any others in the Falklands.

The penguin oiling industry had fascinated me ever since I had found try pots on the coast of Grand Jason. On Steeple Jason I found the remains of many try works along the south coast, and, though the pots used for boiling the penguins down had gone, piles of burnt bones, stone corrals, and the oilers' small stone shelters remained in evidence, showing how vast an industry penguin oiling had been. Rockhopper penguins appeared to have suffered most, as the corals were centred on existing Rockhopper rookeries, and the charred bones piled two or three feet high were rockhopper bones. Records confirmed that the rockhopper was the species most used by the oilers, and I had never seen any mention of a Gentoo's being taken. However, I did not suppose that the oilers had been careful to avoid Gentoos, and, before I left Steeple, I had made a discovery that showed that this species too had suffered.

Making my way to the west end of the island one morning, I decided to walk along the northern slopes of the island's backbone of hills, so that I could look down over the wide plain that stretched along the north coast. Above the Gentoo grounds a low col breaks through the hills, giving an easy route to the south. Coming abreast of this col and looking down towards the Gentoos, I saw something that made me stop abruptly: running diagonally in the direction of the Gentoo colony were two parallel lines of rocks. These lines were spaced about ten feet apart and stretched for over a third of a mile; they were clearly manmade and ran from the colony to the col.

After visiting the site several times, I decided that these lines of stones must have been retaining walls and that they had perhaps marked a route by which rockhoppers had been driven over from the south side of the island to try works in the north. Where the Gentoos came ashore there was a deep gulch that would have made an ideal landing and loading spot for casks of oil, and so it seemed that the oilers had decided that it was better to drive the birds closer to where the oil could be loaded. However, though I thoroughly inspected the area by the Gentoo colony, I could find no sign of a try works thereabouts. The nearest try works, and substantial ones at that, were on the south side of the col. This eventually led me to wonder whether the movement could have been the other way round: whether Gentoo penguins had been driven to try works on the south. The more thought I gave to this idea, the more certain I became that it was right. The Gentoo is quicker and more nervous than the rockhopper, and the oilers might well have taken advantage of its natural instinct to move inland when breeding. When the birds had been rendered down, the full casks of oil could have been rolled down the gentle slope to the north shore, perhaps using the same walled route. This would then have served a double purpose, and all the rendering down would have been done on the south.

I was never able to date the workings near the south side of the col, for, though there were letters about oiling on Steeple and Grand Jason, I knew these workings to be older than those recorded. I spent a great deal of time going carefully through old records of the Colony, gleaning every bit of information on the oiling industry; for I was interested not only in when and how the oilers worked, but also in finding out what the islands had been like before they were violated by man. Unfortunately, there are few records of the Falklands before 1842, when the islands' first civil administration was established.

What is clear is that thousands and thousands of penguins were killed for their oil. The industry reached a peak about 1864, and between 1863 and 1866 a total of 63,000 gallons of oil were brought into Port Stanley for reshipment. Records indicate that the oilers expected to obtain one gallon of oil from eight rockhopper penguins, so in those three years over half a million penguins were rendered down.

Steeple Jason had an unusual type of mouse, which probably had arrived there by accident, in a shipwreck. These mice were quite different from those found on the main islands, having longer tails much larger ears—and a very bad habit of getting into stores! On my arrival on Steeple, I found that they had been into all the emergency supplies left from my previous visit. I thought I had taken adequate care by packing the supplies in tin foil and hanging the boxes from the roof of the hut, but even then the mice had got to the food and ruined it. This was serious, as it left me short of basic foods. Fortunately I had brought a quarter of beef from Pebble Island, but, though I hung it in a place where it was fairly dark and airy, the weather was so warm that I expected it not to last for more than a week. In fact, I ended by eating beef every day for a fortnight, having no option but to do so.

To add to my problems, I had trouble with the radio. I had arranged to contact Carcass every other day, but by the tenth day my signals were getting weak. The signals continued to weaken even though I had a hand generator with me and spent up to three hours each evening trying to recharge the batteries; so in the end I decided to cut contact altogether, in the hope of conserving some energy for the day when the Beaver came. I reasoned that West Point and Carcass would know that if I had trouble and wanted them I could signal in some other fashion. I always carried parachute flares capable of putting a bright light up several hundred feet, and in reasonable conditions these would be visible over thirty miles away.

One night I began to wonder if I might have to use these flares. I was suddenly awoken by a terrific bang on the side of the shanty, and immediately switched on the torch to see what had happened. Everything seemed to be in place, but I was conscious that it was unnaturally quiet for 11.30 at night: no petrels could be heard; not a murmur came from the sea.

I was half out of my sleeping bag when I heard a soft, rising moan of wind. Before I was on my feet, the moan had reached a roar, and the next second the hut had become a punchbag to a violent explosion of wind. Again there was a bang on the side of the hut, and then I realised what it was. To meet the Beaver I had brought a rubber dinghy, which I had tied to a stake a short distance away. Even though the dinghy was weighted down with heavy pieces of timber, the wind had lifted it like a piece of scrap paper and slammed it against the side of the hut.

Hearing another moan, I realised that I was in for a noisy and nerve-racking night. These gusts of wind, or "woollies", as they are called locally, are peculiar to the Jasons. By some phenomenon, probably the shape of the mountains, wind is squeezed into tremendous gusts that, as I saw the day after, are capable of flattening a heavy sea. All night I stayed dressed with essential gear packed, ready to dive for the outside, if need be. What my chances out there might be I could not tell; but I could occasionally hear sheets of corrugated iron being swept along by the wind. These belonged to an old shearing shed that had been ripped apart by such gusts some years before, and it was nothing unusual to find them lying three or four miles from where they previously had lain.

All the next day the winds continued, and through the doorway of the hut I filmed their effect on the sea. The rest of my time I spent recording the wind howl and writing a careful account of the scene.

On 29 October, when the Beaver was due with Len, there was good visibility, no wind, and only a slight swell. I managed to pass a message to Kitty, saying that all was well for a landing; but then the radio failed again. An hour before I expected the Beaver to arrive, I dragged the dinghy down to the shore and paddled out to get a better idea of the swell. Rubber dinghies are fine for some jobs, but I could see that it would not be easy trying to film the landing and keep the boat steady too. Half an hour later I gave a direct call to the aircraft. Ian could just hear me and gathered that I was ready for a landing but not happy with the situation.

Shortly after I had taken the dinghy out again, the Beaver flew low over me and I saw Ian shake his head, then fly on. As it was clear that he had decided to try a landing on the south side of the island I hurried ashore and back to the radio transmitter. Minutes later Ian came through saying that he had found a spot where it was flat calm and had managed to put Len ashore on a rock. From Ian's description I knew that he had landed about two and a half miles from the hut. As I made my way to the spot, Ian flew over low and gave me a grin.

I found Len sitting on the rock, complete with large suitcase. His first words to me were: "What kept you then, lad? Pity you couldn't have been here to film the landing!" However, our problems were by no means over yet: getting Len plus heavy suitcase off the rock, which was awkward to approach and nearly cut off from the mainland, was far from easy. However, I was greatly relieved when I found that the reason why the suitcase was so heavy was that it was half full of tinned food!

Len told me that *Forrest* would be coming out in four days, which left little time for looking round, filming, and catching penguins. Fortunately I had already had some experience of catching penguins, but it was a job that I did not like doing, especially at that time of year. Summer, which is the time when most bird collectors operate, is the breeding season, and many collectors do not know enough about the birds they are collecting, or do not take sufficient care, to distinguish breeding from immature birds. Usually they take the more brightly plumaged breeders, so depriving birds of their mates and chicks of their parents, and causing eggs to be deserted. In an attempt to have this stopped, I had suggested to the Government that collecting should be prohibited in the breeding season, except, perhaps, for the taking of immature birds. However, collection permits were a source of revenue, and my suggestions had no effect.

I had spent a lot of time watching rockhopper and Gentoo penguins and I knew that on the fringes of their colonies were birds that, while behaving like breeders, would not lay that year. Len readily agreed to my suggestion that we collect only birds of this type, and this we did. Later on, in January, the rookeries would be swelled by the arrival of the previous year's young, which, after nearly a year at sea, would return to the colonies fat and in excellent condition, and would remain ashore without feeding until they moulted. Easily distinguished, these one-year-old birds were the ideal ones to collect, but we would not be on the islands when they arrived.

The radio continued to give trouble, and Len and I would sit at the hand generator for hours, trying to build up power in the batteries. I was rather amused one morning to hear communications between Carcass Island, Sedge Island, West Point and the master of RMS *Darwin*. Now that Len was on Steeple, everyone seemed concerned that nothing was being heard from me. There was speculation that Len was ill: apparently Roddy was preparing *Gleam* with the idea of coming out to check; and on top of this, thought was being given to diverting *Darwin* to the Jasons to see if we were all right! "That is just what we need," I said to Len, "and I can see the Falkland Islands Company sending you a fat bill for her diversion!"

I was no radio operator, but I remembered that, when I was with the Army in Jordan and there was trouble in contacting base, the problem was solved by taking the set to the top of a mountain. I decided to see whether this would work on Steeple, and installed the radio on one of the peaks. I got through, but the signal was too weak, and the other side seemed to think that my "All OK" was a call for help. Giving up, I packed the set and trudged back to camp.

Whether it was the journey up and down the hill or the reconnecting of the set I don't know, but, on getting back and trying the charger again, I noticed that the battery indicator had suddenly gone into the "charged" position. Switching on, I called the Marine headquarters and immediately heard, "Where the hell have you been all this time?" "What's my signal like?" I asked. "Good." What had caused the trouble I do not know, but we had made contact only just in time, for next morning *Forrest* would be coming to collect us.

There were no delays in our pick-up, and by the end of the first week in November we were back in Stanley with Len's first collection of birds. On 10 November he sailed with them for Montevideo, from where he hoped to fly them to England. All in all, it had turned out to be quite a successful expedition.

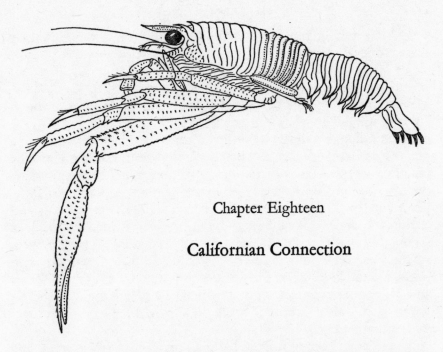

Chapter Eighteen

Californian Connection

In 1970, Annie, the girls and I again spent Christmas on Kidney Island, and spent a lot of time trying to locate the nest burrows of greater shearwaters. On Christmas Eve we waited in the tussac for the shearwaters' arrival, hoping to identify greater shearwaters and find out where they landed. As the main flight of birds started to wheel overhead, I distinctly heard the call of a greater shearwater, which eventually we spotted. Every few minutes it would pass right above us and call, making me wonder if its mate were close by. This was suddenly answered when the bird crash-landed in front of Annie and actually finished up in her lap. After resting for a few seconds, it left her lap and quickly disappeared into one of the burrows that lay between us. The moment the bird was out of sight, the weird calling of a pair of greater shearwaters started from inside the burrow, where we later discovered a newly hatched poult.

On the other side of the island was a rocky bay used by a group of sealion. I thought it worth trying to get some film of the animals with the two girls looking on, as they had shown an unusual knack of moving close to animals. Within ten minutes of arriving on the scene, they were sitting within three or four feet of a cow and yearling seal, who showed no alarm at all. They might even have been able to approach closer, but, obeying my rule of respect to wild creatures, I said that they should not. I got the film I wanted, and also a telling off, for in reloading the camera I accidentally scared the seal away.

May 1971 was to be the delivery date for the manuscript of the book I was writing. The work had gone well, but, in researching into the penguin oiling, whaling and sealing industries, I had accumulated a mass of material, only a small percentage of which could go into the manuscript. I was fairly certain that I could make the delivery date, but saw that, owing to the infrequency of mails between the Falklands and England, there could be long delays over editing and revision. It seemed far better to be in England for all this, and, as Annie was due leave in May, I wondered if this could be managed. At the same time I wondered if we could also make a working trip to the United States. Hal Seielstad felt that I should visit California and by personal contact follow up what I had achieved in the art world, and I also wanted a break and to renew personal contact with a number of conservationists.

Late in 1970 I sent a further batch of paintings to California, and in December Hal wrote saying that he was arranging with Dr Lindsay to hold an exhibition at the Californian Academy of Sciences. Hal wanted me to be present at one of the exhibitions of my work, but I made it clear that this was impossible unless I could cover the costs of my journey. On 29 December I received a heartening telegram from Hal: "All paintings sold; arranging lecture tour June."

A letter followed, explaining that the Academy had bought the entire collection of paintings and that a lecture tour was being arranged in conjunction with exhibitions of my paintings. Already it had been organised for me to hold two lectures at the Academy—hence the telegram. In April a further telegram arrived, saying that Hal had tentatively arranged for six to ten lectures in the area of San Francisco. The subjects would be birds, mammals and conservation in the Falklands, and would yield a minimum of $500 for the series. The telegram ended with "Need your immediate reaction", which Hal got in the simple reply "Excellent news!" This meant that we could make the journey home and to the States, so plans were made for leaving at the end of May.

On 7 June we arrived in San Francisco. It was rather odd meeting

Hal in such surroundings, for, when I had met him four years before, it had been in a forest in southern Chile. However, this second meeting was nonetheless enjoyable, and we spent nearly a month as Hal's guests. During this time we were kept well occupied with the hectic but enjoyable business of lecturing, and, though it was the holiday season and audiences were not as large as they might otherwise have been, the lecture tour was a great success. After seeing the amount of interest shown by people who attended the lectures, I was left in no doubt that wildlife tourism supporting conservation in the Falklands could work.

During that month I met many people who were directly concerned with conservation in the United States. The Sierra Club, Peninsula Conservation Centre, California Institute of Man in Nature, and Committee for Green Foothills were all in some way connected with the lectures and I met many of their members and executives. As an outsider, I was surprised and rather concerned to learn that these groups spent a great deal of time in dealing with administration problems, and that there was a tendency for groups to fragment rather than unite. This was sad, for it meant that a great deal of time that could have been spent in fieldwork was lost in administration.

However, all those I met were obviously dedicated people, and it was a joy to speak to persons who had aims similar to mine. Two such people, Tim and Helen Love, became firm friends of ours, proving of invaluable assistance on the lecture tour. They often travelled over a hundred miles an evening to get us to and from a lecture, and must have known the text of my talks almost word for word.

We spent quite a lot of time at the Californian Academy of Sciences, where we again met Dr Lindsay and Dr Orre. I had contributed an article on seals to the Academy's journal *Pacific Discovery*, and was now asked to write an article on penguins. In addition Dr Lindsay wanted me to meet Tom Tilton, who was a member of the Academy's Board of Trustees and had been interested in my paintings. I don't know what I expected a trustee to look like, but I was surprised to find Tom a young and energetic businessman keenly interested in the work of the Academy. We became firm friends and he later became a keen follower of my projects.

After meeting Tom's family and spending a few days with him and them at their country home on Lake Tahoe, we went on to Washington, and after a brief stay there, continued to New York.

While there, I discussed with Dean Amadon and Dr Murphy the unusual prion that I had found on Beauchêne Island. With only one specimen to study, we could reach no firm conclusion on its species; so for the time being the matter was left unresolved.

From New York we flew to England to see about the book. I had arranged that we should stay with my sister and husband, whose home was set in beautiful country, very quiet, and the ideal place in which to work. This was just as well, as a lot of work had to be done; and the next five or six weeks were passed in cutting and revising the manuscript.

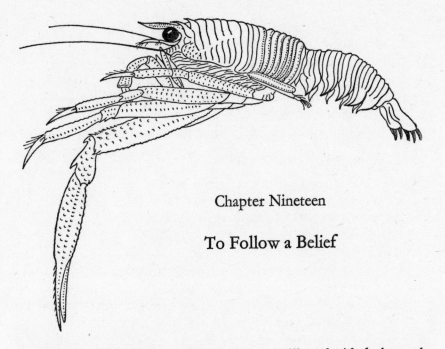

Chapter Nineteen

To Follow a Belief

As Dr Murphy and Dean Amadon were still undecided about the prion discovered on Beauchêne Island, I decided to revisit the island and carry out a more detailed study of the species. This raised again the problem of how to get there; and, as I had already imposed a great deal on the good offices of the Navy, this time I approached the Government to see if I could charter *Forrest*. It was agreed that I could charter her for a diversion, and that a month later she would pick me up again. The problem of communications and of finding someone to go with me was resolved when a Marine, Norman Clark, said that he would like to go, and that he would be able to take a radio transmitter with him.

Our first two attempts at reaching the island were foiled by bad weather, and it was not until 28 December that we succeeded. In the meantime I had formally accepted a Government proposal that I act as an adviser on wildlife and conservation matters. My relationship with the Government had been improving for some time, and I was often called in for discussions. As a natural consequence of this, I was asked to become an official adviser, with a retainer of £50 per annum. I gratefully accepted the position but not the retainer, preferring to act in a purely honorary capacity and so retain full independence.

When we reached Beauchêne Island, we did so not aboard *Forrest*,

but on HMS *Endurance*. Captain Bowden was very interested in the
work I was doing, and had offered to drop me on the island during
the ship's voyage south and collect me on the way back thirty-two
days later. So my fifth visit to Beauchêne Island began, and, though
it was four years since I had last been there, I found the hut intact
and everything in it in place.

Before the *Endurance* left Beauchêne, its helicopters flew round the
perimeter of the island to check for signs of fur seal, which again
were not found; and then made a number of runs down the length
of the island, taking large-format aerial photographs. I hoped to use
these to obtain firm evidence of the size of the albatross and penguin
colony, and so put a stop to the controversy about it.

However, the main purpose of this expedition to Beauchêne was
to gather information on the prions and make a final survey of the
island. Unfortunately, my stay was shorter then planned, owing to
unforeseen complications. On 10 January, while making radio contact with Stanley, I heard from Annie that Len Hill would be
bringing a BBC film team to the Falklands on the 27th. They would
be flying in by Albatross seaplane from Argentina, and asked if I
would arrange for them to land at Steeple Jason and spend a week
there. Added to that, they wanted me to be on Steeple before their
arrival, so that I could give them a weather forecast, film the
landing, and see the aircraft away again. I told Annie that the idea
was ridiculous, which apparently she had already conveyed to Len
over the phone. Giving vent to my feelings, I wrote in my diary:
"This is all very well but (a) I have to get off this island; (b) how do
I get to Steeple to start with; (c) how do I then get back from
Steeple; (d) how do we cope with the Lindblad *Explorer*, which is
due at the same time; and (e) what happens to all my time and the
plans that I had laid for the expedition that I have now started on
Beauchêne?" Finally I wrote, "To sooth my thoughts on all this,
am going up to the Citadel stack tonight to find prions!" This I did,
and, having caught and carefully examined ten birds, was in no
doubt that the birds I had found in 1967 were quite distinct from
the thin-billed prion found elsewhere in the Falklands, and were
breeding in large numbers. This discovery made me feel better, and
gave me the boost I needed in order to be able to give thought to
Len's plan!

The following day it poured with rain, and before long the hut
floor was swimming in water. The weather continued to worsen,
and on 13 January my diary entry read: "What a bloody day this has

been. Woken by a wind that must be over 60 knots from the east-north-east. Spray coming right over the camp site; Norman's tent lost its flysheet. Bitterly cold with showers that developed into a hailstorm." The next day was the same, with winds so strong that the inside of the tent was like a windsock. Every time a squall came over, the wind drove a fine mist spray through the tent fabric, and gradually everything became soaked.

While this weather persisted, I did at least have time to ponder the problem that Len had bounced on me. The first thing I decided was that the idea of landing the Albatross seaplanes at the Jasons was out; and, besides, I could not see that the Government would allow it. On the 14th I learned that Annie had phoned through to England and spoken to Len about this, and that he had said that, if I got back to Stanley, he would meet me there and that we could go to the Jasons by boat. At the same time I heard that the proof of my book on the Falklands had arrived in Stanley.

All this meant that I had to return to Stanley, and for days Beauchêne Island transmitted and received a flow of messages with various plans for getting Norman and me off the island and for organising the proposed Steeple Jason trip. On 21 January *Forrest* arrived to collect us, and so another stay on Beauchêne was cut short.

On my arrival in Stanley I had just four days to prepare for the Steeple Jason visit (which meant collecting supplies and equipment for a team of seven, and organising transport there and back); to make final arrangements for the visit of the *Explorer* (which was due on the same day as Len); and to go through and despatch the book proof!

Two days before Len and the film team arrived, the Colonial Secretary asked me if I could shed any light on the forthcoming visit by Mr Hill's party. We had each assumed that the other knew all about it, when in fact the whole thing had been arranged outside the Falklands. This was made particularly serious by the fact that Len would be using aircraft belonging to the Argentine Navy. To balance the delicate political situation, the Royal Navy with HMS *Endurance* was brought into the operation.

On 25 January, with a day to go before the arrival of Len's party, it was finally arranged with the Government that the two Albatross seaplanes would land at Stanley, and that the six members of Len's group would then transfer to *Endurance* for the voyage to Steeple Jason. After the filming expedition was over, *Forrest* would come out, pick up the team and transport them back to Stanley in time for the return of the Albatross from Argentina. For my part, I had to accompany the Lindblad expedition to West Point and Carcass, then somehow reach Steeple Jason on time to film the others' arrival.

On the evening of 27 January I sailed with *Explorer* for Carcass and West Point, which we reached on the 29th. There I received word that Len's arrival had been delayed and that *Endurance* was only now on her way out to Steeple. Captain Bowden was sending one of the ship's helicopters to pick me up and fly me direct to the island, so that I could just manage to be the first to arrive!

At midday, in the most beautiful conditions, I was put down on Steeple Jason, only to find that the hut in which I had stayed the previous year had gone, and with it essential supplies and items of equipment. Fortunately the wool shed still stood and the water tank was intact and full; but much had gone that we could not do without. Hurriedly I checked a list of the items that had been left in the hut, and scribbled a note for the helicopter's observer. I saw that, if *Endurance* could not supply the main items that were missing, it might well be necessary to cancel the whole scheme.

Once the helicopter had gone, I walked the twenty yards down to the beach. A vast amount of broken timber lay along the tide line, and here and there was the odd rusted tin from the stores. Just offshore among the rocks lay a number of white enamel plates, and on the seaward side of a reef was the main part of the old "Stanley range" stove that had stood in the hut. I could hardly believe that a cast-iron stove that four men had had difficulty in moving had been blown to the far side of a six-foot high reef. The only conclusion that I could draw was that some terrific wind had carried the entire hut to the beach and over the reef, the stove falling free. Checking further, I saw that the wool shed, which was some forty feet square, had been moved bodily some two feet out of vertical. I shuddered to think what sort of wind had caused this havoc, as even the terrible gusts that I remembered from my last stay on the island had left the hut and the wool shed in place and intact.

Minutes later, helicopters arrived bringing Len, the BBC crew and Franz Lazi, a German photographer whom I had met during the *Navarino* trip. For a few minutes the whole scene was pandemonium, with the noise of the helicopters, people running about trying to film the scene, and me trying to find out whether *Endurance* had been able to supply the items requested. When the helicopters had gone and everything had quietened down, I was introduced to the film team, which comprised Ned Kelly (director), Hugh Maynard, Howard Smith and Morris Fisher. Len was his usual cheerful self and glad to be back in the islands, though not too pleased, I found out, about having to come out on *Endurance*. When I told him of the problem it had been to arrange everything, he simply said, "You worry too much, lad".

The team's visit had two objectives: to collect more birds and to film the collecting and the island for a BBC *World About Us* programme featuring Len. While we were on the island, a message detailing which species Len was allowed to collect was passed through from the Colonial Secretary. From the message it was clear that Len wanted to take Macaroni penguins, which I had previously explained to him were too rare to be collected. To take even a few would, in my opinion, set a dangerous precedent, perhaps bringing the species close to extinction in the Falklands. The message to Len stated that his application to collect Macaroni had yet to be approved; and, by a piece of official bungling, a message was later sent to me asking my opinion on the matter. There was only one answer I could give. When my reply was relayed back to Len (all this happening over the same radio) it was with comments to the effect that there were "thousands" of these birds on the north coasts of the Falklands. It was an uncalled-for remark by people who knew no better and was to lead to the break of a friendship.

What had been a comparatively small incident was eventually to have far-reaching effects, and I went to a lot of trouble to prove that what I had said was justified. Finally undisputed evidence was gathered to show that talk of "thousands" of Macaroni penguins on the north coast was ridiculous; in fact, the largest group in this area numbered eleven birds. Exactly how many of these penguins there are in Falklands I do not know, but the largest group I have found in the islands, and the only one that might be termed a "colony", numbers about fifty birds.

My fears about the danger of increased irresponsible collecting had been greatly intensified when I heard that a collector had visited South Georgia at the height of the breeding season and had taken a considerable number of adult king penguins. This was bound to result in the death of many young. I raised the matter with the Government, repeating my suggestions that only immature birds should be taken, and, in the interests of collectors and birds, only at the start of their moult. The Government then asked me what I thought should be done to increase the effectiveness of the Falklands' conservation provisions. The export of birds and animals was one of the points raised and, though I explained that I was not against this *per se*, I suggested that certain aspects should be looked at more carefully. So many problems were involved that the Government decided that for the next two years, while the matter was being sorted out, no further export licences would be issued.

Licence fees for collecting various species had been increased some time before, though not at my instigation, as some thought. In fact, I disagreed with the increase, thinking that the earlier level had been fair to both sides. Particularly ridiculous was the practice of charging collectors a £5 fee for an upland or ruddy-headed goose. Whereas farmers were killing off these birds and actually paying a bounty for their beaks, charges were being made to zoological gardens, trusts and other bodies who wanted to see the species survive!

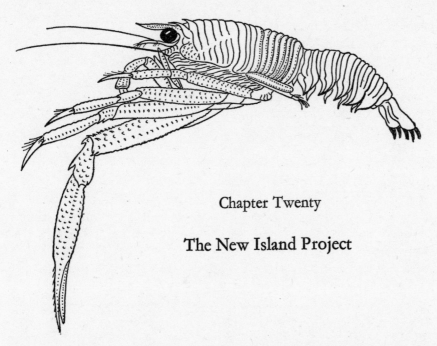

Chapter Twenty

The New Island Project

During my visit to England in 1971 I met Richard Fitter of the Fauna Preservation Society (FPS). From an article I had written for the Society's journal *Oryx*, he had learned something about my plans for reserves in the Falklands, and when I spoke to him I told him that I was sure that a number of smaller islands could be acquired if the necessary support were found. On 21 September he wrote asking for details of these islands and saying that he had a potential donor. In my reply I mentioned one island that I considered had great botanical value and said that I knew of two large islands that would be coming on the market. These, though I did not name them at the time, were New Island and Carcass Island. The former I was particularly anxious to see pass into the hands of some conservation body, for, despite a long history of spoliation, it had vast potential as a reserve.

As regards Carcass Island, Annie and I had discussed with each other and with its owners, Cecil and Kitty Bertrand, whether we could obtain the island and operate it both as a farm and as a reserve. I saw that it would only antagonise the sheep-farming industry if the larger islands were purchased and cleared of sheep, and, besides, I was convinced that the main hope for conservation in the Falklands was to prove that it was economically viable. If the larger islands were purchased as reserves, they would have to be self-supporting, through either farming or tourism or both.

In a letter to Richard Fitter I explained this, and proposed that, if one of the larger islands could be purchased, the island should be controlled jointly by a conservation body and by a group with responsibility for the wardening of and for wildlife tourism on the island. I also said that I thought it important that tourism should be controlled carefully, and that an example should be set to show how conservation and tourism could work together, to each other's benefit.

Richard Fitter wrote back saying that he thought the idea a good one, and that, although he could not see the FPS taking part in such a scheme, thought it should be considered if a suitable island emerged. Later he sent word that the donor of whom he had spoken was willing to contribute up to £1,000 for freehold. This would certainly buy one of the smaller islands, but the two big islands I had in mind would, I expected, cost £16,000–20,000.

Annie and I were now seriously thinking of obtaining Carcass Island, and, as Kitty and Cecil had offered us first refusal, we had decided to take up the offer and try to obtain the capital. During the *Explorer*'s visit in January 1972 (at the same time as the Len Hill trip), I told Lars Lindblad of my hopes of obtaining Carcass and said that New Island was likely to come on the market soon. I had heard rumours that the Falkland Islands Company was showing an interest in the island, and this suggested to me that the company was hoping to cash in on wildlife. Lars, however, thought that I should not worry about other parties obtaining the island, since, if they wished to go into wildlife tourism, they would probably have to look towards the visits of the *Explorer*! At Carcass I briefly discussed with the Bertrands the plans for that island's purchase, and was a bit taken aback when Lars made an offer himself.

At West Point the next day the question of New Island was raised again. Lars was all for going to see the island. I suspected that this had something to do with the fact that Sewal Pettingill, who in 1954 had spent some weeks on the island, was on board; no doubt he had spoken to Lars of the island's beauty and wildlife. What neither of them realised was how the island had suffered since then; and I had a hard job persuading Lars not to go there. For him to have taken a wildlife expedition to the island could have caused complications and would have been an embarrassment to all.

Sometimes, however, I was not so successful in persuading Lars against a certain course of action. During the rather hectic period between the time of my arrival in Stanley from Beauchêne and the arrival of both the Lindblad expedition and Len Hill's team, I had been in radio contact with *Explorer* and had heard that the ship was approaching Beauchêne and that Lars wished to make a landing. I again pointed out the dangers of doing so, and affirmed the Government's decision that no landings were to be made. There I thought the matter ended, but two days later I learned that a landing had occurred. Probably it had been a spur-of-the-moment decision, but I saw it as a bad sign and was worried for the future.

My own future in the islands was far from certain. I had no property in the Falklands and my plans for obtaining Carcass seemed doomed to failure. I was confident that the Bertrands would not sell to anyone who would not care for the island, but this did not solve the problem of my future. As a dedicated conservationist, I was bound to—and had—trodden on many toes, and would have to go carefully if my position were not to become impossible.

This is shown by the fact that I could not openly declare my interest in New Island. The island would be sold to the highest bidder—except, perhaps if that person happened to be me. My interest in conservation had been for years an invisible source of conflict with the owners, and was unlikely to recommend me to them now.

For Roddy, however, the situation was different. For some time I had been suggesting that he should show an interest in the island, the idea being to win the support of an organisation that would take the island as a reserve. During our brief meeting with Lars Lindblad on West Point, Lars suggested that we should try to acquire the island jointly, and asked Roddy if he would go to New Island and discover if the owners would sell. This appeared to me an encouraging step forward, but, knowing that only a few hours earlier Lars had made an offer for Carcass, I was somewhat puzzled and inclined to go carefully, in case the whole scheme fell through.

Calling at West Point on the way back from Steeple Jason, I was able to discuss the scheme further with Roddy. Our discussion, held in a dinghy in the middle of West Point harbour, was something of a turning point, for I explained to Roddy that it was now quite clear in my mind that a move for New Island had to be made at once. Roddy tended to be in favour of waiting until Lars returned later in the month, but I impressed on him the urgency of the situation and the need to establish an offer.

On 10 February I heard that Roddy was going to New Island to discuss the purchase. On the following day I was alarmed to hear from Carcass that it had been stated on the South African news that *Explorer* had gone aground in Antarctica and was in a serious condition. I did not know much about the Lindblad business, but I imagined that the ship was a vital part of it and that the company could ill afford for the vessel to go out of service. This being so, it seemed that it would be a long while before Lars was again in the Falklands, and that he would no longer wish to take part in the purchase of New Island. On the 12th I wrote Roddy a long letter on the problem, but again emphasised that we should go ahead regardless.

For the next twelve days we were in a state of anxiety waiting for news about *Explorer*, word from Lars about New Island, and word from Roddy about his talks with the island's owners. It was now clear that much bigger concerns were interested in New Island, and I knew that if we made one mistake we would lose our chance. On 18 February Roddy came into Stanley to say that we had first refusal, but that he was worried about the ship and the possibility that Lars might no longer be interested. I was convinced that whatever happened we should still go ahead, and was sure that, if we were given the chance, we could raise the capital. However, Roddy had told the island's owners that he would let them know one way or the other the following week, and it appeared that other offers would be made on the coming Monday. As Saturday had already gone, the only way we could contact New Island before Monday was through unofficial channels. By this means it was arranged that the owners of the island would fly into Stanley on Monday, and on Wednesday a legal agreement for the purchase was drawn up and signed. Obviously we had made it just by the skin of our teeth, for later a complaint was made that we had used unofficial channels for relaying a business message to New Island.

Now that we had a signed agreement we were able to breathe again and take stock of what we had let ourselves in for. The agreement was fair and allowed some deferment of payment, but the staggering fact was that we now had to find £28,000. £10,000 was the first payment, and towards this Annie and I contributed every penny of our small savings. The second payment, £8,000, was due in a year, and if it could be met would secure the island definitely. A year seemed plenty of time in which to find the money, but I realised that we had no room for complacency.

As nothing had been heard from Lars Lindblad, I wrote to him on 23 February explaining that we had gone ahead with the purchase of New Island, and hoped that he would be able to take an interest in the island's development as a wildlife reserve and attraction to wildlife tourists. At the same time I wrote to Dr Jungius, then Conservation Officer of the WWF in Switzerland, and told him of the project, saying that I hoped that the WWF would wish to assist. In similar vein, I wrote to numerous other people who I thought would be interested. Among these were Richard Fitter of the FPS (to whom I wrote, "It never rains but it pours!"), Tom Tilton of the Californian Academy of Science, and Sam Lebovitz of the Lebovitz Foundation. Mr Lebovitz had taken part in one of the *Explorer* trips, and, after hearing a lecture I had given on conservation, had told me that, if ever I required help in my schemes, the Foundation might be able to assist.

As Roddy was already the owner of a considerable property, and might be disastrously affected if our scheme for purchasing New Island ran into financial difficulty, we agreed to establish what was to be called the New Island Preservation Company, with limited liability. On 13 March 1972 the company came into being, with Roddy and me holding equal shares. The aims of the company were stated in its Memorandum as being

To assist and encourage the scientific study of the wildlife of the Falkland Islands and to promote tourism in the Falkland Islands of a nature conducive to the stimulation of interest in Falkland Island wildlife and its preservation and the doing of all such other things as are incidental or conducive to the attainment of this object.

and

To carry on business as farmers in such a manner as to prove its compatibility with the preservation of wild life.

Shortly after the company had been formed, I produced a project description giving in more detail what I hoped could be achieved with the island. One of my main hopes was that New Island would serve as a base for ornithologists and biologists working in the Falklands.

In my letters to the FPS and WWF I stated that, if they could assist us in overcoming the next and most critical payment, we would undertake to operate the island as a reserve. The New Island property included, in addition to the main island, six small offshore islands, and I suggested to Richard Fitter that the FPS take these as security for any loan that it could let us have.

Suddenly we received a telegram from Lars Lindblad saying that he was willing to participate one-third in New Island. This created rather an awkward situation, as by this time we were having serious negotiations with the WWF and FPS and had received word that the Lebovitz Foundation would consider helping us and that the Californian Academy of Sciences also was interested. As we had agreed that the island should be run primarily as a reserve, and as we wished to avoid too strong a commercial involvement, I thought it best to continue current negotiations.

Early in April I wrote to Richard Fitter informing him that I now had the option to purchase for the FPS three small islands elsewhere in the Falklands. In May he wrote back saying that the FPS would take the small islands, provided that these could be vested in the Society for the Promotion of Nature Reserves (SPNR). This was the first time that I had been directly concerned with the Society, although I later had a lot to do with it and its Chairman, Christopher Cadbury. Of New Island Richard Fitter wrote that, at one of the meetings of the FPS council, a member had said that he understood that the sum required to complete the purchase had already been raised, from other sources. At about the same time I heard that it had been advertised in South Africa that Lindblad Travel had now purchased an island in the Falklands. All this was quite wrong and I was at a loss to know how the rumours had started; but it meant that I had to write to everyone again, to put things right.

By June I was still busy with correspondence to the FPS, WWF and Mr Lebovitz. In a letter from Dr Jungius I was asked what attitude the Falklands Islands Government took to the establishment of New Island as a reserve. I knew that, if we had taken New Island and declared that we would remove all sheep from the property, the opposition would have been tremendous; but, as it was our intention to run the farm and reserve together, I could not see that any complaints would be raised. However, though the Government was aware of the project, it did not have full details; so in June I placed these before the Governor, E. G. Lewis. Mr Lewis thought the project interesting, and said that, if we wished to give the island sanctuary status under Falkland Islands law, he would recommend the Council to give its approval.

In July I heard from Richard Fitter that he had discussed with both the IUCN and WWF the problem of raising funds for New Island. There was now a WWF–IUCN world biotope fund from which grants could be obtained, though not for land that would be held by private individuals. Also, given the rather unstable political situation in the Falklands, it was felt that grants would be forthcoming only if the land were held by an internationally respected organisation.

Shortly after, I had to report to the FPS and SPNR that the owner of the three small islands that I had been trying to obtain for them had suddenly changed his mind and now wished to hold them. This, of course, had no direct bearing on the New Island project, but I was afraid that it would undermine the societies' confidence in my ability to carry this project through. As a result, I began to think of going to England to discuss the matter at a personal level.

On 24 July I received a telegram from the FPS to say that the whole £8,000 needed for the next payment on New Island could probably be made available, provided the island were vested in trustees or the SPNR, but not individuals. I had been thinking of forming a trust to look after the scheme and Mr Fitter suggested the same. Roddy, who fortunately was then in Stanley, agreed with the plan. For Annie and me it mattered little that we would not be part-owners of the island; but, as we had sunk all our capital into the purchase we had to have a reasonable assurance that we could operate the venture ourselves.

After receiving the telegram from the FPS, I finally decided that I must go to England to discuss the whole situation. Unfortunately, this was no easy matter, as RMS *Darwin* had now been withdrawn from service. As part of a new agreement aimed at easing political relations between Argentina and the Falklands, Argentina had agreed to provide the islands with an external air link and to assist in the construction of an airstrip. Until this was ready, the only regular link with the outside world was the Albatross seaplane flown into Stanley every fortnight by the Argentine Air Force. Seats on this aircraft were almost impossible to come by, as there was room on board for only seven passengers.

We now had a new Colonial Secretary, Mr Layng, to whom I explained the New Island project and its problems. He obviously was interested in the scheme, and, besides supporting the project in a letter to the WWF, helped me obtain a flight out of the colony.

I was due to fly out in mid September, so in August the first main meeting of the New Island Preservation Company was held. We all agreed that the island should be placed under some sort of trust and that I should act on behalf of the company in negotiations with the WWF, FPS and SPNR. It was an important meeting, and some vital decisions on the future of the island were made.

On the evening of 26 September I arrived in London, and the following morning I was at the offices of the FPS. In phoning round and discussing the New Island project, I found that the earliest date for which a meeting of all parties could be arranged was 19 October; so for over three weeks I was kept wondering about what the final outcome would be. In fact the meeting, at which the FPS, SPNR and WWF were represented by Richard Fitter, Christopher Cadbury, Ted Scrope-Howe and Nigel Sitwel, turned out to be something of a disappointment, as it seemed that it would not be easy to reach agreement on the form the trust should take.

While in London, I stayed with a young couple, Susi and Renato Zannatta, whom I had met on one of the *Explorer* expeditions and who shared my interests and would have loved to have worked in the islands. On returning from the meeting to their home in Islington, I found that they had guests: William Pitt and his wife. After I had been introduced to them, Susi asked me about the meeting and I explained what had happened, saying that what I needed was a lawyer who specialised in trusts. This last remark brought laughter, and William offered his services! He and I discussed the problem extensively, but in the end it was decided that the best solution was for the New Island Preservation Company to let the SPNR hold the island in trust, and for the SPNR to give the company a long lease on the island, with conditions to suit both parties.

Later in my stay in London, I had a phone call from Sam Lebovitz who after saying that he thought the Lebovitz Foundation could assist the project, asked if I would go over to New York to discuss the matter with him.

The following day I had yet another long-distance phone call: this time from Annie in the Falklands. She explained that wool prices were rising very rapidly and that wool brokers were negotiating prices for the next season's wool clip, something never known before in the islands. The Falkland Islands Company was acting for the brokers, and already agreements had been reached with all the main farms. However, as a certain amount of secrecy had been employed, Annie had only just learned about the sales. Partly because of this, she was determined to negotiate the best possible price for the New Island wool, and turned down offers of 74 and 79 pence a kilo—themselves very good prices. Thanks to Annie's insistence on negotiating, we later obtained a price of 82 pence a kilo, which was a higher price than many larger farms with better wool had secured! All this was in some ways an amazing stroke of luck, for when we had agreed to purchase New Island, wool prices were at their lowest for years and nobody would have bought a farm for what wool might bring. However, though this unexpected change meant that financial assistance was no longer so critically required, I believed it essential to continue with my plans for having the island placed under a trust, so ensuring its future as a reserve.

On 2 November I left London for New York, and a few days later I met Sam Lebovitz in the lounge of La Guardia airport. Again the interest and the keenness to help the project were there, but the Lebovitz Foundation would have preferred to have taken sole interest, which would have meant that other organisations could not participate.

Also while in New York, I discussed the situation with Lars Lindblad, who repeated his wish to take a share in the island. However, I explained that I thought it best to place the island under a trust, and that he could best help the project by assisting in the establishment of a small wildlife tourist business. Later I met up with Lars in Buenos Aires, where we discussed the possibility of establishing a small lodge to accommodate tourists on New Island. Carcass was again referred to, and Lars confirmed his interest in its purchase.

Returning to the Falklands, I felt that, though I had not accomplished everything, the trip had been a success. Most important, I had returned with the basis of an agreement for the New Island project. The WWF International had approved it as an international "A" project and had allotted a token grant of £1,000. The WWF was also prepared to loan £8,000 interest free for one year—the amount needed for the next payment on the island. The SPNR had agreed in principle to hold the island in trust and lease it back to the New Island Preservation Company for ninety-nine years. There were numerous points that had yet to be ironed out, but I felt we were now close to establishing the Falklands' first international reserve.

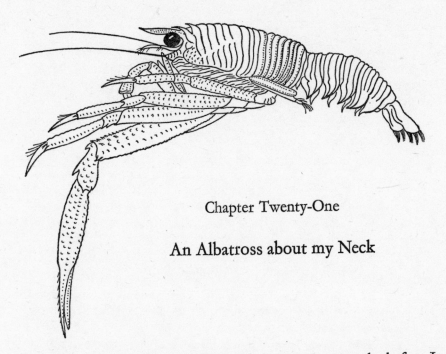

Chapter Twenty-One

An Albatross about my Neck

Following my return to the Falklands it was some weeks before I was able to speak to Roddy on the latest proposals for New Island, and when we did meet I found that his views on the project had changed. I was also sad to discover that the guanaco sent to West Point had been shot, having jumped at and hurt someone. All in all, it was a disappointing time; and, at the next meeting of the New Island Preservation Company, it seemed that the idea behind the company's formation had collapsed.

On 25 February I had to write to the FPS and SPNR to say that it was no longer possible to carry on as planned. This left us in the very critical situation of having to find £8,000 for the payment due the next month—unless, of course, I was prepared to agree to a large commercial business coming into the project, which I was not. There was one other possibility: that the six smaller islands on the New Island property be given to the SPNR and FPS against a loan of £8,000. It was still agreed that these islands should become reserves, so, with the approval of the New Island company, I put the suggestion forward to Richard Fitter and Christopher Cadbury. On 8 March, with the deadline for the next payment only twenty days away, I received a telegram saying that the FPS was willing to give £2,500 for the six islands, but could not offer the rest without security.

That would probably have been the end of the scheme, if it had not been for the fact the island's wool clip had been brought forward, and now had a guaranteed value of several thousand pounds. Obviously, the deal could not be concluded until after shearing; but the brokers' agents were prepared to allow us an overdraft, which, coupled with the offer made by the SPNR, gave us the £8,000 needed. Thus, on 28 March, just two days before the deadline, New Island was finally secure in the hands of the New Island Preservation Company. It was ironic that this had been made possible by the very industry from which I least expected help and with which I had often been at odds, but it was nonetheless a happy conclusion to the matter. I felt that, for the first time in over 150 years, the island could breathe again.

New Island, with its sheltered deep-water harbours, had been discovered and named by American whalers from ports such as New Bedford and New York. It became a base and wintering place for them, and was much frequented while they worked about the Falklands during the early nineteenth century.

In the New Island harbours whales would come to calf, and thus became the prey of these men. On the top of one of the high cliffs at the back of the island, I came across an old lookout point, from which a commanding view of the sea could be obtained. It was not difficult to visualise whalers watching there for their prey.

Many penguins and fur seal also were taken. Sealers fired the tussac to drive out seal; on the penguin rookeries, rough stone corrals were built, and into them thousands of birds were herded, then killed for the try pots. Vast numbers of penguin and albatross eggs were collected; goats and pigs were left to fatten on the island; and sheep and cattle had grazed there for many years. In the process, the island's wildlife had been sadly depleted and a great deal of vegetation had been destroyed.

Yet, despite all, much had survived the rape, and I now hoped that the island would start to recover. How much had been lost for ever, it was impossible to say; but something might be retrieved.

One thing that gave me hope for the future was that the six smaller islands included in the New Island property were to pass into the hands of the SPNR, under the management of the FPS and with me acting as warden. However, when a conveyance was being drawn up, it was discovered that two of the islands, Ship and Cliff Knob, were not listed in the deeds by name, even though they were shown on the New Island property maps. Who then owned them?

New Island had farmed Ship Island for as long as people could remember, and small Cliff Knob had never been of interest to anybody. As it had already been agreed to hand the islands over to the SPNR, an embarrassing situation was created, and only the very good relationship that I now had with the Government helped remove further complications. In April the Governor issued us with a Crown grant for these two islands, and on 30 December 1973 the six became the property of the SPNR.

New Island's involvement with tourism remains small. For a few years now, we have allowed access to a small number of visitors, who have come from as far afield as Europe, North America and South Africa. Through this we have learned a great deal about the problems of keeping tourism in harmony with our conservation aims, and also about what our visitors are seeking. I hope that soon we can progress to the next stage of the project, and establish the island as a centre for research into the bird and animal life of the Falklands.

An island for which I have a very special concern is Beauchêne. It was only after many years of struggle that I was able to get the Government to agree that the island should become a strict nature reserve and not open to tourists, and even after that the struggle was not quite over. In a small war of correspondence about the refusal to let tourist boats visit the island, I was one of the targets, and the whole question was referred to the British Government. Only when the battle was over, and it had been confirmed that Beauchêne would be made a strict reserve, did I discover that the war had been started by people whom I would have expected to be allies, rather than opponents, in the struggle to avoid damage to this very valuable island. It was good that the island's future was being secured, but sad that that final battle should have been necessary.

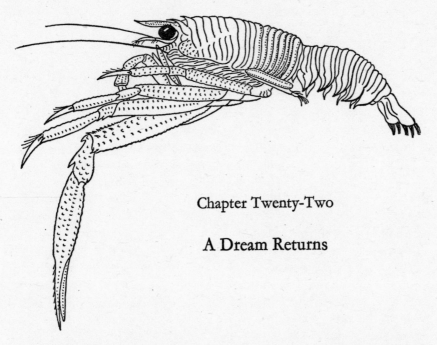

Chapter Twenty-Two

A Dream Returns

In the last ten years the Falklands have made considerable strides in
the field of conservation. Although we still have a long way to go,
a far more enlightened view about such things is now prevalent, and
there is a willingness to bring in experts from abroad to advise on
conservation problems. A marine biologist was brought in to investigate the problems that might arise from harvesting kelp in the
islands, and even the matter of the upland goose is now under pro-
fessional investigation. The establishment of reserves and sanctuaries has become a reality, some thirty islands and areas of mainland
being designated as such. Some are Government-owned, some come
under the SPNR, and many are privately held, but all are helping to
ensure that the Falklands' "stockpiles" of wildlife are not squandered.

Now that an air link has been established between the Falklands
and Argentina, the islands are much less remote than they were.
This has in many ways been of great benefit, but it has also opened
the Falklands to less desirable influences that it will not be easy to
keep in check.

For many years it has been known that the rich seas about the
Falklands are of great potential value to the fishing fleets of other
nations. It had been accepted that these waters would have to be
used in man's search for food, but I argued that we should lay
plans and make careful investigations before the search began. Cer-

tain areas would have to be protected so that we should not experience the same problems as had been caused by fishing activities
off the Peruvian and Chilean coasts. Now it seems that our seas are
rich in other things, and there is even a whisper that oil may be
found off our coast. Already the search for these riches has begun;
but I believe that there is still time to make the necessary plans.

Unfortunately the conservationist always has to prove his state-
ments with hard facts, which are not always easy to come by. Time
brings proof in the end, but so often this comes too late, when the
damage is already done. Following that, the mistake is quickly forgotten. However, now that ways of improving the Falklands' pastures are being sought, perhaps people should be reminded of the
lush pastures that existed before man started to burn and overgraze.
Those who were involved with the whaling industry should think
of the millions of pounds' worth of vessels that now lie abandoned,
remind themselves that it was they who ran themselves out of
business, and ask themselves whether it would not have been wiser
to have limited their activities, so that there would still be whales
enough to farm.

We are told that we cannot exist unless we can pay our way. This
is perhaps true; but, by the same token, we cannot exist if we destroy
our means of survival. There must thus be a compromise between
economics and nature. Conservation I have always maintained
should be economically viable, hence the attempts to put it on a
firm basis through wildlife tourism. But it would seem that even
this is in danger of being swept up into the net of big business.

Living as we do in these islands, we live in a mini-world. We see
on a small scale what is bigger and more remote in the world at
large: the struggle of politics, business and economics. Sometimes
the scene is frightening, like that of a recurring nightmare that
becomes a little more real each time it is repeated.

Index